A GARDEN STYLE BOOK

HEIRLOOM GARDENS

[SIMPLE SECRETS FOR OLD-FASHIONED FLOWERS AND VEGETABLES]

MIMI LUEBBERMANN

PHOTOGRAPHY BY FAITH ECHTERMEYER

CHRONICLE BOOKS

SAN FRANCISCO

Library of Congress Cataloging-in-Publication Data:
Luebbermann, Mimi.
Heirloom gardens : simple secrets for old-fashioned
flowers and vegetables / by Mimi Luebbermann ; pho-
tography by Faith Echtermeyer.
          p.   cm.
"A Garden Style Book."
Includes bibliographical references (p. 106) and index.
ISBN 0-8118-1451-3 (pbk.)
1. Flowers—Heirloom varieties.   2. Vegetables—
Heirloom varieties.   3. Fruit—Heirloom varieties.
4. Gardening.   I. Title.
SB407.L84 1997
635—dc20   96-38866
                        CIP

Printed in Hong Kong

Cover and interior design by
Aufuldish & Warinner

Distributed in Canada by Raincoast Books,
8680 Cambie Street, Vancouver, B.C. V6P 6M9

10 9 8 7 6 5 4 3 2 1

Chronicle Books
85 Second Street
San Francisco, CA 94105

Web site: www.chronbooks.com

DEDICATION

To those individuals who have ever saved and nurtured a seed, respecting its history, loving its individuality, and appreciating its future. In particular, to Craig Whealy of Seed Savers Exchange and to the other fine nonprofit organizations, seed banks, and plasma exchanges. They quietly, out of the spotlight, have dedicated their activities to saving our history and preserving plants' genetic future for all of humankind. To them goes our appreciation and respect for their tireless efforts that most often go unnoticed, underfunded, and ofttimes unappreciated for their truly awesome and divine work.

CONTENTS

POTTED HEIRLOOMS FOR INSIDE   42

POTTED HEIRLOOMS FOR OUTSIDE   52

HEIRLOOMS IN A PATCH OF GROUND 68

FROM THE GARDEN TO THE KITCHEN 86

Bury your head in the satiny-soft petals of old roses lyric with heavy perfume or watch giant sunflower heads trace the sun's

daily path. In your hands, cradle beans, brightly splashed with splotches of burgundy red and dried to marble hardness. Set out night-fragrant white nicotiana in containers next to your favorite sunset perch. Relish the names of love-in-a-mist, 'Deer's Tongue' lettuce, lamb's-ears, johnny-jump-ups, love-lies-bleeding, and bachelor's buttons, knowing that the seeds of these beloved plants have been bequeathed to modern gardeners from the past, handed down over time.

¶Treasured by our ancestors, these handed-down plants—annuals, perennials, shrubs, and trees—were passed along (hence their designation as "pass-along" plants) through the generations because their flavors sang out; gardeners waited for the scented blossoms to stir the air; the strong, vigorous, and reliable growth created a joyous beauty or a usefulness that improved life. These plants in our gardens give us a glimpse of our ancestry, an almost indefinable sense of those who gardened before, like us, digging their fingers into the warmth and richness of the soil to sow, grow, and then to save the seeds for next year's pleasure.

¶Time-faded spidery handwriting in old diaries details the often torturously difficult journeys from homeplaces to the America of immigrant dreams. Diary entries tell of small snips—taken from a plant near the old doorway—that were coaxed to set down roots in the new home place, much as did the immigrants themselves. Immigrants slipped seeds into the country: Seeds sewn in hidden places in clothes, from hatbands to hems, were a desperate act of smuggling to bring the old along to the new land.

¶Edible plants have a special place in heirloom gardens because food and culture are so intertwined. The new citizens brought seeds of familiar food plants with them to the strange new place, not sure how else to survive without the staple foods of their culture and cuisine. Often because of their honored part in a festive meal, a religious day feast, or simply the closely woven ritual of the harvest seasons, plants and seeds came along to the new land as important reminders of the old land. Typical examples of food plants brought to the new country can be found in ethnic markets— grain to grind into flour for traditional Ethiopian injera bread, beans for the nourishing and delicious frijoles of Mexican cuisines, or a Thai basil to bring an essence of the homeland to a strange land. Gardeners in the United States are lucky to live in a garden melting pot.

¶The business of selling seeds started late in the nineteenth century, and in the United States, the Shakers were one of the first groups to package seeds for sale. At that time, individual groups or companies grew plants, improving the varieties and saving the seeds of the plants with the best characteristics. They also began experiments with some crossbreeding, taking pollen from one desirable plant and using it to pollinate another member of the same family. Sports, plants that suddenly appear in a garden or field (the 'mortgage lifter' tomato, for example), were lucky accidents of nature that gardeners carefully nurtured by saving the seeds every year. The growers would always pick the strongest plants with the heaviest production for the seed parent.

¶Hybridizing started early in the twentieth century, after Mendel's laws of genetics revolutionized the world of plant breeding. Plant breeders crossed plants in such a way that they created mules, plants that could not subsequently breed true. They have seeds, but when planted, many of these seeds do not germinate, and those that do burst to life follow the

traits of one parent, usually looking totally different from the original plant. Hybridizing allowed the breeders to create plants with added disease resistance, higher yield, and a different shape and color of bloom.

¶ With the advent of the refrigerated railroad car, the produce business started to boom, with potatoes grown in Idaho rushed off by train to New York, Florida oranges hustled up to Chicago, New England asparagus whistled down to New Orleans, and of course, tropical flowers from the South shipped up to the North.

¶ Suddenly, shipping factors influenced the kind of flowers, fruits, and vegetables that were commercially viable and, thus, lucrative. Roses were developed for their tight bloom shape and the length of time they stayed furled—enough to get from field to boudoir; tomatoes and peaches needed to stay hard until they sat on the kitchen counter, perhaps as long as two weeks after picking. Hybridizers at one point even dreamed of a square tomato, all the better to fit into the packing box. Flavor and fragrance were forgotten in the mad rush to breed commercially economical varieties for the high-production factory farms.

¶ For many home gardeners though, saving seeds of the plants they had always grown seemed more satisfactory than buying the highly touted new varieties that grew successfully but just didn't live up to the proven reputation of the old family favorite. The disease resistance and added yield of the hybrid didn't make up for the qualities that were missing. Scentless roses and tasteless tomatoes were some of the plants that didn't make any sense to these dedicated home gardeners. Roses were supposed to have fragrance that on one sniff, made the world's troubles seem farther away. Tomatoes needed the sweet-tart flavor of summer's sun to mark the season.

¶Some plants had special characteristics that made them worth saving: perhaps an apple that stayed on the tree long past the first frosts, and kept in the storeroom until January snows; a rose that bloomed earlier than any other rose; a tomato that fruited despite a cold summer; and a cucumber that was more prolific than any other. Certain plants did well in sandy soil and others adapted to survival in heavy clay. Some smaller mail-order companies continued to sell heirloom seeds, but more and more of the hybrid types worked their way onto the pages, as more and more of the older seed types began to disappear.

¶Gardeners are a generous lot; perhaps the abundance of Mother Nature inspires the sharing of seeds and plants that seems to be the essence of gardening. From even a few seeds, plants grow, divide, and multiply, so handing a thimbleful of love-in-the-mist seeds over the back fence to a neighbor seems an ordinary gesture. This sharing impulse has resulted in a heritage of seeds cherished and saved by home gardeners. Collectors sprang up who realized the importance of maintaining stocks of old-fashioned varieties that were being lost as old-time gardeners died. Rosarians hunt in old cemeteries and abandoned farms for rose varieties—long thought disappeared—that are planted on graves or along rickety fences. Seed banks and germ-plasm repositories now collect, catalogue, and protect this priceless heritage.

¶Plants, both wild and domestic, are disappearing all over the world. Like certain wild animals impacted by human overpopulation and loss of habitat, this dwindling number of plants means a lack of diversity and a smaller genetic base to draw from when breeding new plants and maintaining healthy populations of current plants. For example, during the Irish potato famine of 1845, most of the potatoes planted in Ireland were one particular variety, called a 'Lumper', that was brought to Ireland some two hundred years previously. Consequently, when the disease hit, it wiped out 75 percent of the potato crop, because it was all genetically

the same stock. Had different types been grown, some might have had a genetic resistance to the disease and survived it, and the million people who died in the famine might have been saved.

¶Different plant varieties have different genetic susceptibility to disease and weather and growth patterns. Plant breeders, when the genetic material is available, have the greatest opportunity to breed plants that can survive disease, stand up to different climates, and prosper with healthy growth and a heavy harvest. Maintaining stocks of all types of plants is the best defense against a future that includes the unknown challenges of feeding a growing population.

¶Yet, all of this conservation may not touch the home gardener who enjoys growing large, meaty black beans the size of giant limas because of the vigor of the vines, the extravagant harvest, and the pleasure of the plate. The ritual of saving and storing seeds goes with the growing of these plants. Many gardeners have devised a system of seed envelopes, neatly marked with names and dates, to store for next year's garden. Some plants happily self-sow their seeds, dropping them conscientiously to grow again carelessly the next year. But for those plants that don't reseed, the gardener's judicious harvesting, threshing, sorting, and storing of the very best seeds neatly marks the end of the season with a promise of next year's harvest. Of course, careful storing, far from bugs or mice hungry at midwinter, guarantees that next year's seeds will be ready to set out.

¶I'm not sure when I, as a young gardener, began to explore the mystery of seeds. I vaguely remember windowsill milk cartons, cut in half, filled with the rising heads of sunflowers planted too close and jostling each other for  room. As proud as a parent, I hovered over zucchini and pumpkin plants that sprang up and out of their containers. As a new gardener, I admit shamefacedly to gathering poppy seed heads from a public park in Anacortes, Washington, and although some of the heads were too green, enough seed survived to start a collection of poppies that I kept for many years, admiring the glorious pink crepe petals in summer, and in fall saving the seed pods in brown paper bags. Newspaper spread over the table caught the seeds as we cracked open the heads, after shaking out as many of the seeds as we could. Big jars seemed always, miraculously, to hold enough seeds for friends with some left over to sprinkle on breads and salads.

¶I became the recipient of plants from other people's gardens; friends and relatives shared their favorite plants with me. A friendly neighbor gave me an egg carton planted with seeds of bachelor's buttons. My mother-in-

law gave me lunaria seeds, the silver dollar plant, which in my mild-winter California garden, came up as early purple spring blooms to decorate my garden patch, and, in small glass bottles, decorated my Easter table. The children cut the silver-dollar-sized pods to use as play money. Self-sowing after their cheerful branches of silver dollars waved in late summer's breeze, the plants reseeded for the next year. Whenever I see lunaria, I recall with pleasure the kindness of my mother-in-law, who gave me my first garden manual and encouraged my beginning efforts with a gift of lunaria and a sampling of plants from her own garden.

¶Someone else gave me love-in-the-mist seeds, advising me to toss them out and forget about them. Like a carpet, they spread, taking over a garden bed with their blossoms of pink, white, and blue, year after year gradually changing until blue-only blossoms came in early summer.

¶My children grew sunflowers, and harvesting the large pumpkin-wide heads was our farming activity in a tiny city garden. As other gardeners before me, I carefully tilted handfuls of seeds into old envelopes, sealing, labeling, and then storing them in a big old can on a pantry shelf.

¶Now, admittedly, I am a bit more sophisticated from years of trial and error, reading, and study. I try to protect the purity of some of my plants with bagging and careful selection. And I have become a plant archivist, casually asking older gardeners whether they have any special plants they treasure, and shamelessly asking for cuttings. Recently, I discovered a flowering cactus that had belonged to a great-grandmother; bits of the leaves were stuck into potting mix, rooted, and were passed on to grateful grandchildren. I angle for invitations to meet older Italian or Portuguese farmers with large family gardens, just in the hope of finding another interesting vegetable or flowering plant.

¶I grow a towering row of sunflowers, just one variety to maintain purity—black oil—for my rabbits and the wild bird visitors. A patch of 'Lumina' pumpkins spreads on one side of the garden, and the squash, 'Rouge d'Etampes', and the blue-skinned winter squash are set far away on the other side. I bag—here in dry-summer Northern California I can use grocery bags—the 'Lumina' blossoms to prevent cross-pollination but don't worry about the other types. Those seeds I buy yearly. In the wild back part of the garden overlooking the sheep pasture grows teasel, recalling the early Spanish missionary fathers.

¶Love-in-the-mist blooms every spring, left to self-sow, although I save some heads, crushing them between my fingers and tossing them over the bed in the fall, just in case. I cut off the round heads of my breadseed poppies, Papaver somniferum, low down on the stalks to leave long stems. After I shake out the seeds, dried upside down in paper bags, I give away the handsome dried pods and the delicious seeds. Wrapped in rice-paper packets, they become presents for relatives and friends. Strolling through my garden, I feel the company of many other gardeners, nodding their heads in satisfaction at the size of the sunflowers, the colors of the poppies, the gleaming corrugated rounds of pumpkins.

¶This year I want to add more old-fashioned roses, redolent of the perfume that the Persians collected—attar of roses—and some China roses, which I can imagine were visited by lords and ladies in rustling silks and twirling fans. The Tulipa batalinii, bulbs from the slopes of the Mediterranean hills, like little orange packages; rainbow-colored beans from Africa; cacti from South America; herbs from Asia—all these burst into beauty in my own private Eden, telling me tales of past gardens or of adventures in other lands. Gardeners are lucky travelers to be able to reach back into time and across to other lands simply by working the soil in their own gardens.

CHARACTERISTICS OF HEIRLOOMS

Heirloom plants, longtime companions in our gardens, vegetable beds, and orchards, can be annuals, biennials, perennials, shrubs,

or trees. Annuals are quick-growing plants that sprout, flower, set seed and die in one season. Starting with seeds means you have a mature plant in about six weeks. Nasturtiums and squash are two examples of annuals. Biennials grow to maturity and die back in two years, with growth in the first year and flowering and seed in the second. Perennials grow, flower, and produce seed, but they continue to flourish for at least two years, or much longer. Perennials can be deciduous, losing their leaves in the fall, like roses, while others, such as rosemary, stay evergreen.

¶Although there is no definitive agreement on the definition of heirloom, most collectors and growers consider heirloom plants as those plants under cultivation in gardens for at least one hundred years, which can be propagated year after year by seeds, cuttings, or divisions.

¶Heirloom plants, unlike hybrid plants, are either self-pollinating or open-pollinated. A self-pollinating plant has the innate ability to produce seeds without obtaining pollen from another plant. An open-pollinated plant must have pollen from its own or another similar plant brought to it by insects, birds, or humans to create seeds. When seeds are formed, if they are harvested and planted, they will sprout and grow, reproducing the parent exactly.

¶Unlike the self-reproducing, open-pollinated plants, hybrid plants have been cross-bred to emphasize certain features or characteristics such as disease resistance or increased productivity. In order to achieve this, hybrids have been bred to two parent varieties, usually themselves inbred. Seeds from hybrid plants are consequently sterile in most cases, but if they do sprout, the plants no longer represent the parent. You must buy new hybrid seeds to plant every year.

¶Many catalogues and seed companies now clearly label seeds as heirloom types, and note carefully whether they have been hybridized—but the term *heirloom* is applied loosely. Breeders will hybridize an old-fashioned plant and still use the original name. Generally, it's best to request open-pollinated plants, or to ask whether the saved seeds can be sprouted the following year.

¶Open-pollinated plants can be pollinated with pollen from other varieties. If you are growing sweet corn next to popcorn, and pollen from the popcorn pollinates the sweet corn, the resulting seed shows the effects of the cross-pollination—kernels will not be true to the parent seed. Those plants that do not reproduce the seeds of the parent plant probably have crossed. See "Saving the Seeds of Heirloom Plants" (page 37) for tips on avoiding this problem.

¶Heirloom plants, grown in your garden for several seasons, adapt to your soil and your climate and begin to prosper based on those quite specific conditions. Localized adaptation is one of the advantages of gathering seed and replanting the same variety year after year. Plants accustomed to living in your garden handle the vicissitudes of climate and soil better than those tender plants used to living in ideal, and quite unreal, nursery conditions.

¶Planting your garden with heirlooms provides a wider variety of color, texture, and shape in flowers, fruit, and vegetables than can be found in the marketplace. Choices of purple beans and purple artichokes, funny looking green or striped tomatoes, or flat pumpkins make your garden an exciting place.

¶Taste and fragrance are other attributes of heirlooms. The exquisite flavor and texture of edible varieties come from years of gardeners selecting for taste, without considering commercial shipping needs. Many fruits and vegetables ripen quickly or perish within days, meaning a fine harvest for the gardener but not for the greengrocer, who needs tough produce that can hold up for days waiting for customers.

¶Yet, there are some heirlooms that may not do well in your garden. Hybrid tomatoes carry inbred disease resistance to fungal and soil-borne diseases as well as to those pesky under-the-ground nematodes. In some gardens, old-fashioned roses become covered with black spot and rose rust, and hybrids, bred to be resistant to these diseases, grow successfully, blooming their heads off. If you have these problems with your garden soil, use hybrids when planting in the ground, but grow heirlooms in containers filled with sterile soil. Or, because heirlooms have the ability to adapt to local conditions, try the plant for several seasons before seeking out another variety that may adapt more successfully.

ABOUT GROWING HEIRLOOM GARDENS

There is one caveat about growing old-fashioned plants. Heirloom plants, precisely because they have not been hybridized—and therefore do not have improved disease resistance and vigorous growth—may, in some cases, need more coddling and watching over. Although with other heirlooms, you can plant them and then sit back and enjoy the results. Careful cultivation and attention to matching the plant with your garden environment will overcome many difficulties.

¶Vegetable plants like tomatoes and potatoes, in particular, are susceptible to soil-borne diseases, so planting in different beds each season is recommended. Additionally, working in copious quantities of organic compost, with the beneficial action of its microorganisms, can boost healthy growth. If plants don't do well in your garden with its own recipe of soil and climate, try a different variety, which is not really a hardship considering how many excitingly different and delicious varieties there are. Above all, don't give up. Keep notes and continue to try out different varieties of plants, garden locations, watering requirements, and soil mixtures. If you have any problems, call the nursery or mail-order catalogue where you bought your plants and discuss them with the staff. Their technical support can assist you in analyzing and solving any difficulties.

WATER

Water carries nutrients from the soil up through the roots and stem to the leaves. As water evaporates through pores in the leaves, the roots draw more water from the soil, like straws sucking up liquid. During periods of high evaporation, such as hot or windy days, the rate of water loss from the leaves increases, so the roots need more water. When the leaves lose more water than the roots can quickly replenish, the plant wilts. A properly watered plant is one that has constant access to readily available water in the soil. When temperatures soar, make sure to increase your watering.

¶Soil composition affects the amount of water available for plants and the health of their roots. Very sandy soil drains quickly, so plants have less water available; clay soils drain less readily but may not be good for plant roots. The air in the spaces between soil particles contains the same gases as our atmosphere does; the roots need the oxygen to breathe. When soil is filled with water, oxygen is pushed out and consequently is not available to the roots. Just as plants can die from too little water, they can die from too much. Normally when an area of soil fills with water, gravity pulls the water down through the spaces between the soil particles, allowing oxygen to fill them again. Certain factors, such as heavy clay soil, the lack of a hole in a planting container, or a layer of rocks at the bottom of a planting container, prevent proper drainage, and plant roots suffocate. Even though it is traditional to add rocks or crockery to the bottom of containers, they can stop drainage, so ignore that century-old instruction and just fill the container with potting soil.

¶Adding plenty of organic matter to your garden beds before you plant is an excellent way to improve healthy water penetration and retention. In sandy soils, the organic matter retains moisture; compost absorbs water like a sponge, holding it so it is available for the plant roots. In clay soils, the compost breaks up the clay particles, creating spaces through which water can drain and oxygen can refill.

SOILS AND POTTING MIXES

Soil is a mixture of three particles—sand, silt, and clay—plus any organic matter. The silt, clay, and organic matter interact with soil water and provide nutrients to the plant roots. Sand, although chemically inert, also plays an important role in plant health. The largest in size of the particles, sand creates correspondingly large spaces between the soil particles, which contributes to fast drainage, high oxygen concentrations, and good vertical water movement.

¶The organic matter in soils is mostly old plant material decomposing under constant attack by bacteria and fungi, which over time liberate mineral elements that are essential to plants for their growth. The bacteria and fungi also benefit plants by fighting off microorganisms that cause plant diseases.

¶A good garden soil crumbles easily in your hand. Healthy soil has a rich earthy smell because of its organic material. Your soil should have this good smell, and you should see small bits of decomposed compost among the grains of soil when you look closely. Your spade should slide into the ground easily, and water in a planting hole should drain out slowly but steadily. Good soil produces good plants, so if your plants are not growing well and you do not see signs of disease or insect problems, find out from your local nursery where you can have your soil tested.

¶For container plantings, use a good-quality potting mix to ensure it retains moisture, drains well, and does not become concrete hard in late summer. Commercial potting mixes have been sterilized, which makes them cleaner than decomposing materials for growing plants indoors.

PREPARING THE GARDEN BED

For garden beds, prepare the soil two to three weeks before your seeds or transplants are ready to set out. If the soil is so wet that it falls off the shovel in clumps, you will have to wait to get started until the soil dries some or risk compacting the ground, making it rock hard. Compacted soil has less oxygen, so the roots suffer from oxygen deprivation and your plants do not grow successfully.

¶First remove existing plant material such as weeds or plants that you no longer want to grow there. Add 4 inches of organic compost, and with a shovel, a spade, or a machine such as a rototiller, turn over the soil to a depth of 12 to 18 inches. Water the turned soil and allow any undesirable seeds that may be in the ground to sprout. When the ground is damp but not soggy, remove the unwanted plant material once again. Using a hoe or shovel, break up any clods and rake the surface smooth for planting.

FERTILIZERS AND pH BALANCE

The major nutrients needed for plant growth are nitrogen, phosphorus, and potassium (N, P, and K). A plant removes these nutrients from the soil and uses them to grow. Adding fertilizer to the soil replaces the missing or used-up nutrients, allowing the plant to continue its growth. Because nutrient needs are greatest during periods of rapid growth, fertilize your beds when you are preparing them for planting.

¶Commercial fertilizers list their contents as the percentage of each nutrient, in the order of nitrogen–phosphorus–potassium. For example, an NPK formula of 10–10–10 has equal amounts of nitrogen, phosphorus, and potassium. You may want to consider using organic fertilizers in your garden. Choose the new brands with NPK formulas, or use a combination of bonemeal, bloodmeal, wood ash, and fish emulsion to build up the fertility of your soil. Some gardeners prefer all-purpose slow-release organic fertilizer granules, added before planting, to a liquid fertilizer that needs to be applied twice a month. Try the different methods to find one that works best for you. Although there have been no conclusive studies, there are a number of testimonials to the improved taste of vegetables that are organically grown.

¶Plant growth also depends upon soil chemistry. The pH (potential hydrogen) balance of the soil affects how well a plant absorbs nutrients from the soil. Acid soils have a pH of 6.9 and lower; alkaline soils have a pH of 7.1 and higher. Check with your local nursery to find the special products to test your pH level, and then add appropriate amendments to improve the pH of your soil.

Seeds

Starting your own heirloom plants from seeds is easy, and it offers you the advantage of growing a wide range of varieties that nurseries do not regularly stock as small plants. If you live in a cold climate with a short growing season, starting seeds inside produces vigorous plants that are ready for transplanting when the ground warms up. Seeds also can be sown directly into the ground later, after the warmth of spring has brought the ground temperature up to a level that encourages germination. Whether you plan to sow indoors or outdoors, order your seeds in January for spring and summer sowing to make sure you start with fresh high-quality stock. (Some seed sources are listed on page 105.)

¶Check your nursery for the choice of seed starting kits, such as Styrofoam flats, plastic six-packs, or peat pots. Choose pots or containers with individual sections for each seedling so that the transplants will pop out of them easily. Milk cartons, egg cartons, and plastic containers can be recycled to work just as well.

¶Seeds need temperatures of between 65° and 75° F to germinate. Some gardeners place electric heat mats underneath germinating trays to keep the soil evenly warm. A sunny south window may provide enough warmth and light. If your plants lean toward the light source and look spindly and weak, they are not getting enough light. Hang grow lights or full-spectrum lights 4 to 6 inches above the containers for strong, sturdy growth.

¶Start your seeds six to eight weeks before you want to put plants outside into the ground or into containers. You can buy potting mix or you can make your own with equal quantities of vermiculite, perlite, and peat moss. It is important to use a sterilized mix to avoid diseases that infect seedlings. To make sure the plants get off to a good start, add all-purpose, slow-release organic fertilizer granules to the mix according to the directions on the fertilizer container; or when the seedlings are 1 inch high, water them once a week with a low-nitrogen fertilizer diluted to half strength.

¶Thoroughly moisten the mix with water, then fill the container to within 1 inch of the rim. Check the recommended directions on the seed packet to sow the seeds at the correct depth and spacing. After you have sown the seeds, pat down the mix firmly and water carefully so you don't dislodge the seeds. Keep the mix moist but not soggy to discourage fungal infections. Place the seed containers where they get four hours of

bright sun a day. If the seedlings begin to look leggy, they are not receiving enough light, so try grow lights or another, sunnier location. When roots begin to show at the bottom of the container, the young plants are ready to be set out-of-doors or picked out and moved into larger containers if you are not yet ready to set them out. Do not let your plants become potbound, because this retards their growth.

TRANSPLANTING YOUNG PLANTS

Young plants raised indoors or in a greenhouse are tender, so accustom them to out-doors before you set them into the garden—this process is called hardening off. For one week before you plant the young plants, set them outdoors during the day only. Start them in the shade, gradually moving them into the sun. When you plant them, do it in the late afternoon, to lessen the stress caused by the heat of the day.

¶To transplant, gently tap out the little plant from its container, taking care to keep the root ball and all its potting mix intact. Check the required spacing for the plants. Make sure to leave enough room so plants do not become crowded as they mature. Make a hole in the planting bed and set in the plant so the top of the root ball is level with the soil. Tamp down the soil firmly around the root ball, making sure the plant is set securely into the ground. Water often until the plants become established and show new growth.

CONTAINER PLANTS

Many small plants grow perfectly in container gardens on fire escapes, small balconies, or even rooftops. Keeping plants watered is the most persnickety job in container gar-dening. A potting mix formulated for containers holds water better than does regular compost, which is formulated as an amendment for garden soil. A drip system will help regulate watering, but if that is not possible, try to water your containers on a regular schedule. If the weather becomes windy or hot, increase your watering and use a fine mister at least once a day on the leaves of the plants. Check the soil dampness by poking a finger down at least 2 inches into the soil every two weeks. The size and shape of your container affects your watering schedule: Plastic containers retain moisture longer than do unglazed ceramic or pottery containers, and plants in small containers get thirsty before plants in large ones.

¶Plants in containers, often in sterile mix, have no source for nourishment. Add all-purpose, slow-release organic fertilizer granules to the container when you pot, and keep up a regular bimonthly routine of fertilizing after you water with a soluble fertilizer, diluted to half strength.

FROST PROTECTION

Gardeners use the words *hardy* and *tender* to roughly distinguish how well a plant withstands cold. Tender plants may be damaged by cold temperatures, and a freeze may kill them. Hardy plants stand up to a certain amount of cold and are often described as hardy to a certain temperature—for example, "hardy to 32° F." Half-hardy plants will usually survive a cold spell, but may not survive extended cold weather.

PESTS AND DISEASES

Quantities of creatures compete with the gardener for a share of the bloom and harvest. Edibles destined for your household's meals must make you cautious about pesticides and herbicides. Try the new series of organic soap-based pesticides that suffocate pests with fatty acids harmless to people and animals. Look into some of the biological controls, such as lacewings and trichogramma wasps (very tiny and not like their larger stinging relatives), which attack plant pests without bothering you. Consider using *Bacillus thuringiensis* (BT), a bacteria spray that kills caterpillars without leaving any harmful residue for humans. Although protecting your harvest by organic methods may be more labor intensive, a safe and productive garden for yourself and your family is a clear incentive.

¶In moist climates, slugs and snails can become very persistent. Look for bait specially formulated for vegetable garden use and put it out in small containers such as empty juice cans. Alternatively, maintain a vigilant watch, going out in the evening with a flashlight to handpick the slugs and snails; place them in a tightly tied bag and discard it in the garbage.

¶Viruses and fungi also attack plants, creating stunted, sometimes unusually colored growth. As soon as you notice any small infected plants, make sure to pull them out and discard them into the garbage. Strip off infected leaves of larger plants and watch them carefully. The best protection against soil-borne fungal diseases comes from mixing into the soil generous quantities of organic compost, which encourages beneficial microbes. If soil-borne diseases persist in your garden, consider growing heirloom plants in containers or raised planter beds filled with sterile soil. Discard the soil if disease strikes again.

Saving the seeds of heirloom plants

The last garden task of the season, harvesting seeds, brings an added moment of joy to the gardener. The pride of stewardship lies in the jumble of seeds in the palm of your hand. Saving your own seeds has a distinct advantage, as well. Plants grown for several seasons in the same garden adapt to their home garden, improving their ability to flourish in the microclimate and in that specific garden soil.

¶In the cycle of the garden, plants grow to maturity, blossom, bear seeds in fruit like berries or tomatoes, in dry pods like peas or beans, and in flower heads and seed pods like love-in-the-mist. The gardener selects the best plants, those which grow the largest, appear to have the most plant vigor and health, and picks out the loveliest fat fruits, pods, or seed heads to save. Woe be to those who gobble up the best seed or harvest the most gorgeous flowers and use the puniest to continue their harvest. Crops and blooms will become smaller and weaker year after year, and may eventually succumb altogether. Because the seeds from each plant of the same variety have a slightly different genetic code, pick fruit or seeds from three or more plants to save for the widest genetic base.

POLLINATION

Pollination is the first step in seed production. Unlike humans, plants carry both male and female reproductive organs, sometimes both occurring in the same blossom, as in a lily, or sometimes, as with squash, in separate male and female flowers. The male part is called the stamen, with one or more hairlike filaments, at the end of which is an anther, which produces the pollen. As the anthers ripen, they split open to expose the pollen. Pollen, carried by the wind, insects, or even the gardener's paintbrush, lands on the stigma. Each grain of pollen immediately produces a pollen tube that grows down the style into the ovules within the plant's ovary to produce the seeds.

¶Self-fertilizing plants, such as beans and lettuce, don't require external fertilization, and in some cases, can be depended upon to produce pure seed without assistance. However, the gardener trying to maintain purity should still observe plant separation to assure purebred seeds.

¶Fertilization becomes a critical issue for gardeners who wish to save pure strains of their heirloom varieties. If you grow several different varieties of corn, the plots of each variety must be isolated from the others in order to avoid cross-pollination. If you are growing 'Lumina' pumpkins and minipumpkins in the same patch, cross-pollination may occur, and the resulting harvest the following year could be very disappointing, depending on which plant's genes win out. The seeds formed from a cross-pollination look different, so you know the first year that your strain is no longer pure.

¶For those wishing to grow more than one variety or those gardening in the city, some simple steps can be taken to maintain the purity of your seed. Remember contamination can come from your neighbor's garden, for the wind and the bees don't recognize property lines. You can separate your plants from each other, setting the plots at a distance, preferably with taller plants or shrubs in between, but for some plants, that may mean as much as a mile apart—not practical for most gardeners. For those with smaller gardens, try planting varieties with different maturity dates. For example, planting different varieties of sunflowers successively a month apart allows them to flower and set seed separately.

¶Should weather factors interfere with your plan so that both the early and the late season variety start to bloom simultaneously, you may need to resort to bagging one type in order to achieve purity of the other. *Bagging* means covering the flowers with a cloth or paper bag, closing the bottom tightly, so they aren't pollinated by the wind or insects. Plain paper bags work successfully only in areas with dry summers, for in rainy areas they become soaked and disintegrate. Order specially treated bags that hold up to the weather from garden suppliers (see Mail-order Sources, page 105).

¶Hand-pollinating followed by bagging works on squash and pumpkins. Using a clean, dry paint brush, brush off pollen from the anther of a male flower—the male is just a flower with no indication of fruit—of the same variety or from the anthers on the same plant and brush it on the stigma. In the case of tomato flowers, you need a small brush, though giant sunflower heads call for a larger brush. After you have pollinated, bag the head of the pollinated flower, making sure to tie the base of the bag securely to prevent insects from crawling up inside.

¶Some dedicated heirloom gardeners fashion large, light cages with a fine-mesh wire top and sides so they can water or the rain can trickle in, but insects and foreign pollen are kept out. Tightly planting the same varieties in beds covered by cages prevents cross-pollination. Row covers from specially fabricated cloth can achieve this same effect as long as they are securely fastened at the ends and sides. Care must be taken because in hot spells, you cannot lift the edges to allow the heat to escape. Using row covers works successfully with spring and fall harvests, when the weather won't cook your plants.

WET PROCESSING

The seeds develop either in a wet fruit, like a tomato or squash, or in a dry seed pod, like a bean or poppy. For each, there are different techniques to separate seeds.

¶For seeds from pulpy plants, open the fruit and scrape out the seeds and pulp. This mixture must sit for several days to allow fermentation to occur, a natural process in which the protective microorganisms cleanse the seeds of many diseases that can affect next year's plants. After the time has elapsed, add an equal portion of water to the mixture. Seeds that float are not viable, so skim them off. Then, in a fine sieve, drain off the seeds; run the water vigorously over the seed mixture to wash away the pulp. Drain the seeds as thoroughly as possible, using a paper or cloth towel to wipe the bottom of the sieve. Turn the seeds out into a glass, ceramic, or metal dish, not paper, which sticks determinedly as the seeds dry. A fiberglass window screen elevated about an inch or two above the surface works admirably, allowing air to circulate around the seeds. Dry the seeds in a warm place, but don't try an oven, direct sun, or any location where the temperature rises above 96° F, because the seeds die at high temperatures. If kept too moist too long, the seeds may actually germinate or be attacked by fungus.

DRY PROCESSING

Podded seeds like peas and beans or seeds in husks can be left to dry on the plant. However, sometimes, in case of impending frost or unseasonable rain, you may need to uproot the whole plant and hang it in a protected, frost-free dry space to allow the seeds to ripen and dry fully. When you husk or shell the seeds, be careful not to crack or break the seeds. Blow off the bits of shell or chaff and store the seeds. Corn can be strung on the cobs, the husks pulled back and the silks discarded.

STORAGE

Seeds are living things, breathing and waiting to grow. Storage techniques keep them alive, and in many cases, they stay viable for years. Your seeds will be happy as long as they are kept dry and in an area of even temperature, safe from bugs or rodents. Baby-food jars, canning jars, or envelopes all work successfully as long as they stay dry—moisture encourages fungal diseases or may cause the seeds to prematurely sprout. Your seeds are a delicious food to other creatures, and you must protect them accordingly. Sad is the gardener who discovers the empty husks—a seed cache carefully gathered that has been breakfast for a mouse family.

RECORD KEEPING

Record keeping assists the gardener by safekeeping invaluable knowledge of plant sources and plant success, and sometimes failure, and growing techniques and requirements. With heirloom plants, as with many of your other garden plants, note briefly the source of the plant (catalogue, neighbor, nursery, or garage sale), the date you received the plant, how successfully the seeds germinated, the productivity of the plant, and the last growing season. If you give seeds to other gardeners, be sure to keep track. If you lose your harvest, you can beg back a start for the next year.

P O T T E D

HEIRLOOMS

FOR INSIDE

Gardeners with not much outdoor space or those who just love having plants inside can grow a variety of heirloom plants indoors quite successfully. After all, the Victorians brought half their garden inside, draping windowsills, growing cabinets, and tables with plants. They even fastened small growing boxes to the back of mirrors so that live ivy could gradually creep over the frame. ❧ The plants suggested here for growing indoors need at least four hours of direct light to thrive inside. Find a sunny windowsill but check the light as the seasons change lest the sun becomes too hot for the plants. South- and east-facing windows usually are the most successful for these sun-loving plants. If you have a patio or fire escape, let the plants sit outside in part shade for several months during the summer, but water them regularly as the potting mix dries out faster outdoors. ❧ Don't be content with just one plant, but create a whole potted garden inside, with shelves holding several pots of one kind of plant. Nasturtiums can grow in a variety of containers, from colorful imported olive-oil tins to old coffee pots, as long as there is a drain hole. ❧ Don't be afraid to put plants temporarily in locations where they don't normally thrive. Try placing the lemon-scented geranium in the bathroom, even if it is dark, and after several weeks of enjoyment, bring it back out to the light. Place the rosemary next to your chair in a puddle of sun, and smell the piney fragrance; or let the lace-cap hydrangea decorate your bedroom. Keep enjoying your plants by moving them to different locations and regrouping them.

ROSEMARY TOPIARY

Rosemary, in forest green with fresh looking needle-shaped leaves, now comes entwined in topiary shapes just the right size for perching near a sunny windowsill. Long revered for the aromatic essence of its leaves, rosemary has been a fixture in medicine chests and culinary herb bottles for centuries. In fact, it is the stuff of myths: the Virgin Mary spread her blue cloak over rosemary, transforming the flowers to their true blue. ¶ Rosemary is best known as the herb of remembrance. Throughout the Middle Ages, brides gave it to their bridegrooms as a token of fidelity, and rosemary was added to bridal cakes. It was often grown in graveyards and added to funeral bouquets. ¶ The strongly fragrant oil in the leaves has made it nature's best air freshener. Branches were added to the rushes covering the floors in halls, churches, and meeting places, to mask other odors. Try warming sprigs of rosemary in the oven or simmer them with juniper berries on a warm radiator in winter if you want a lively and instant fragrance that doesn't come out of a bottle. Sprigs dropped into a steamy bath stimulate and refresh both body and spirit. ¶ Of course, in the kitchen, rosemary pairs well with any meat or vegetable. The taste is hardy, so use it in judicious amounts to keep a balance of flavors. Try finely chopped leaves in breads and fruit desserts as well.

¶ **HOW TO DO IT** ¶ Place your rosemary topiary in a sunny window. Prune regularly to help keep its shape, using the clipped leaves in cooking or bathing. Place the container where it receives four hours of sun a day and keep the soil just moist but not soggy. Fertilize every two weeks with a soluble organic fertilizer diluted to half strength. If you have a suitable location, let the plant summer outside for several months.

Rosemary
Rosmarinus officinalis

What You Need
Potted topiary
Soluble organic fertilizer

Growing Conditions
4 hours direct sun inside,
summer outside in part shade

Hardiness
Hardy

Propagation
By cuttings

When to Plant
Anytime

Lace-cap Hydrangea

The old-fashioned hydrangea has long earned a place in outdoor gardens since it was discovered growing wild in the Americas and Asia. A lace-cap was the first hydrangea seen in Japan by Carl Peter Thunberg in 1775. As an indoor potted plant, a lace-cap hydrangea provides large-leafed, showy greenery and the reward of long-lasting white flowers. Lace-cap describes the dainty flowers, so different from those of the better known mop-headed variety. The flower head contains small fertile flowers in the inner circle surrounded by large outside flowers that have no stamens or pistils and, consequently, are sterile. The flowers are followed by cup-shaped fruit, which gives the hydrangea its name: in Greek, hydro means water and angeion means vessel. ¶ Although the seeds will sprout, it is so easy to start cuttings, any time of year, that most gardeners simply keep a flat going. When you trim or shape your lace-cap, cut the trimmings into 4-inch-long pieces, the bottom of each one cut just below a leaf. Then, remove all the leaves and dip the bottom inch of the cutting into a root hormone powder. Have ready a container filled with moist sand. With your finger or a pencil point, make a hole 2 inches deep for the cutting. Carefully place the cutting into the hole, making sure not to brush off the powder. Pack the sand around the cutting, and keep the container in a shady spot and continually moist. After four to five weeks, test the cuttings by gently tugging at them. Resistance indicates they have sprouted roots. Repot the rooted ones in a container filled with potting soil. ¶ **HOW TO DO IT** ¶ Place your lace-cap hydrangea where it receives four hours of direct sun a day and keep the soil just moist but not soggy. Fertilize every month with a soluble organic fertilizer diluted to half strength. If you have a suitable location, let the plant summer outside for several months.

Lace-cap Hydrangea
Hydrangea macrophylla or H. aspera

❧

What You Need
Potted plant
Soluble organic fertilizer

❧

Growing Conditions
*4 hours direct morning sun inside,
summer outside in part shade*

❧

Hardiness
Hardy

❧

Propagation
By cuttings

❧

When to Plant
Anytime

❧

LEMON-SCENTED GERANIUM

Myth has it that geraniums were created when Muhammad, the founder of Islam, hung his coat on a bush while he said his prayers. Retrieving his coat, he discovered that the plant had turned into a geranium. Victorian women doted on collections of different scented geraniums, placing them inside close to doorways where their long skirts swept against them, envigorating the air with their fragrance. The pungent lemon essence makes the lemon-scented geranium a choice plant to grow indoors. Rubbing a leaf between your fingers will make you almost swoon with the rich bit of lemon. Station the plant in your house where you can brush the leaves as you go by. ¶ Although commonly called geraniums, these plants are actually pelargoniums; they lack the large cheerful flowers of true geraniums. The small pinkish flowers are insignificant, for it is the leaves that please. The plants are very easy care and need little attention except for regular watering and feeding. Make cuttings from the plant in the spring and fall, snipping off three inches of stem to just above a leaf nodule. Many cuttings root in water, so you can have plants to share with your other gardening friends or to enlarge your collection. There are many other scented geraniums, from lime to apple, rose, and peppermint, so you may expand to other fragrances at any time. ¶ Although the leaves can be a great pleasure in your bath, the plant outshines itself in the kitchen. A leaf at the bottom of a plum jelly imbues it with a hint of lemon. Placed at the bottom of the cake tin, a subtle lemon taste imparts a special flavor to the cake. Leaves added to the sugar bowl make a lemon sugar, and of course, steeped in hot water, a gentle, soothing tea. ¶ **HOW TO DO IT** ¶ Place your lemon-scented geranium in the sunniest window. Prune regularly to help keep its shape, using the leaves in cooking or bathing. Place the container where it receives four hours of direct sun a day and keep the soil just moist but not soggy. Fertilize every two weeks with a soluble organic fertilizer diluted to half strength. If you have a suitable location, let the plant summer outside for several months.

Lemon-scented Geranium
Pelargonium crispum
❧

What You Need
Potted plant
Soluble organic fertilizer
❧

Growing Conditions
*4 hours direct sun inside,
summer outside in part shade*
❧

Hardiness
Hardy
❧

Propagation
By cuttings
❧

When to Plant
Anytime
❧

Cheerful nasturtiums

Nasturtiums are another New World plant taken back to Europe after the Spanish conquest uprooted them from Peru. *Nasturtium means a "twist of the nose," from the peppery jolt in the edible leaves and flowers, which are, incidently, packed with healthy doses of vitamin C. Known also as Indian-cress, the leaves and flowers have the flavor of watercress, a relative, and provide a peppery bite in salads. In fact, salad fanciers from the eighteenth century on knew to nibble the succulent leaves and brightly colored flowers. Recipe books exhorted cooks to add flowers and leaves to salad bowls. Even the seeds, pickled in a strong brine to resemble capers, can be eaten.* ¶ *Start seeds early in spring, sowing them into a hanging basket in a sunny windowsill. Avoid the hybridized nasturtiums; find, instead, open-pollinated types such as the handsome variegated leaf 'Alaska' or the 'Empress of India'. Remember to leave some flowers out of the salad and on the vine to form seeds for your next planting. Plant a second pot midsummer for autumn blooms.* ¶ **HOW TO DO IT** ¶ Before planting, soak the seeds in water for two to four hours. Fill the container with potting mix to within 2 inches of the rim. Add 1 tablespoon all-purpose, slow-release organic fertilizer granules and toss with the mix to blend it evenly. Water the mix until it is thoroughly moist. Space the seeds evenly around the rim of the container, about 2 inches apart, setting them down 1 inch into the mix. Pat down the surface and water to fill in any air pockets. Place the container where it receives four hours of sun a day, and keep the soil moist but not soggy.

'Alaska' or 'Empress of India' Nasturtium
Tropaeolum majus 'Alaska' or 'Empress of India'
❧

What You Need
Package of seeds
Hanging container 14 inches in diameter and 8 inches deep
Potting mix
All-purpose, slow-release organic fertilizer granules
❧

Growing Conditions
4 hours direct sun
❧

Hardiness
Tender annual
❧

Propagation
Seed
❧

When to Plant
Early spring
❧

POTTED

HEIRLOOMS

FOR OUTSIDE

If we imagine old-fashioned plants set in brightly colored flower beds flowing alongside smooth-as-croquet-court lawns, cross-mowed to checkerboard perfection, we might faint with envy. Most of us have neither the inclination nor the space to keep up acres of Versailles-like garden brilliance. Should you long for such, head off to your nearest tended public park, and in the meanwhile, enjoy your own treasures neatly tucked up in containers. ❧ Container gardening has much to recommend it. Plants in containers can be showered with attention when in their finest seasonal bloom; you can position them to be admired from indoors or out. When the blossoms are spent, another plant coming into bloom can take its place, providing you with a show all year long. Your favorite garden bench or outdoor reading nook makes a fine site for one or a dozen containers that you can admire when you pause for a moment or a morning's reflection.

Containers with fragrant flowers should be placed where you sit or pass by regularly—an outdoor breakfast table or the path to the front door. ❧ Containers help to foil the weather. Plants with delicate blooms that might be damaged by pelting rain can be moved to a protective overhang. Tender plants in cold-winter areas need to be protected over the winter. Make sure to move them to a space that furnishes plenty of bright light or direct sun and keeps appropriate temperatures. ❧ Situate your pots in a place easily accessible to water. Providing enough water for potted plants on a regular basis is often a challenge. Check plants regularly by pushing a finger down into the potting mix to test the amount of moisture under the surface. Remember that extra hot or windy weather increases their watering needs, so be ready to water more frequently during those times. Mulching your potted plants with 2 inches of organic compost keeps the water from evaporating as quickly. ❧ Don't ever become bored with your display of plants. Imagine yourself a window designer and your grouping of plants, on show. Try varying the heights; mix and match different colors of containers and shades of foliage. Above all, make sure to have a burst of year-round color to liven up your perspective.

NOISETTE ROSE

Roses, so beloved through the centuries, should be a part of everyone's garden. There are hundreds of wild roses, but garden roses have been developed from about twelve different types, all of them growing north of the equator. From time immemorial gardeners have cultivated roses, as is evidenced by dried blossoms found in the tombs of the Egyptian pharaohs, by the poetry of the ancient Greeks and Romans, and by paintings throughout the ages. Roses have particular ceremonial and religious significance in celebrating life, acknowledging death, and pledging eternal love. ¶ With such a history, everyone should have a rose to grow. If you thought you couldn't grow roses because you have no flower beds, think again. Noisettes are particularly desirable for their perfume, their summer-long blooms, and their capacity to adapt to container growing. ¶ Dating back to an 1802 musk-China cross by the John Campneys of Charleston, South Carolina, noisettes display the fragrant clusters of blooms typical of musk roses and the continuous blooming habit of China roses. They were named after the Noisette brothers, French nurserymen who took the seedlings back to Europe. The different varieties come in shades of pink, pure white, and, sometimes, yellow. Unlike most roses, they are tender in freezing temperatures, so place your potted rose in a spot where temperatures stay above freezing during the winter months. ¶ **HOW TO DO IT** ¶ Before planting, submerge the transplant in its container in a sink or bucket of water until air bubbles cease to appear. Fill the new container with potting mix to within 2 inches of the rim. Water the mix until it is thoroughly moist. Gently remove the rose and its potting mix from its container, and plant it so that the top of the root ball is level with the surface of the mix. Fill the hole with mix, packing it gently around the roots. Pat down the surface and water to fill in any air pockets. Mulch the rose with organic compost spread 1 inch deep. Place the container where it receives four hours of sun a day, and keep the soil moist but not soggy. Fertilize every month with a soluble fertilizer diluted to half strength.

'Mary Washington' or 'Natchitoches' Noisette Rose
Rosa x noisettiana
'Mary Washington' or
'Natchitoches'

❧

What You Need
Container plant
Potting mix
All-purpose, slow-release organic fertilizer granules
Organic compost
Soluble fertilizer

❧

Growing Conditions
4 hours direct sun

❧

Hardiness
Hardy to 32°F

❧

Propagation
Stem cuttings

❧

When to Plant
Year-round

❧

FEVERFEW

Feverfew is one of the medicinal plants oftimes mentioned in the early books as a panacea for fever and headaches. Old books variously prescribe sipping a tea made from steeping the leaves or even nibbling them between two slices of brown bread for relief of fevers or migraine headaches. Other books, catering instead to the long life of garments, suggest drying the leaves for sachets that repel insects. Regardless of its use in the medicine cabinet or the closet, this charming perennial should have a place in your garden all summer long. The small, 1/2-inch daisy flowers bloom continually without much fussing. A plant set in at springtime grows to be a large 2-foot-wide and 2-foot-tall perennial by summer's end. Delicate fernlike foliage in light chartreuse is found in some cultivars, such as 'Aureum' or 'Golden Feather'. ¶ *Feverfew, able to withstand frost and not too particular about watering, spreads easily from self-sown seeds. You can also make divisions from large clumps of plants.* ¶ **HOW TO DO IT** ¶ Before planting, submerge the transplant in its container in a sink or bucket of water until air bubbles cease to appear. Fill a new container with potting mix to within 2 inches of the rim. Add 1 tablespoon all-purpose, time-release organic fertilizer granules and toss with the mix to blend evenly. Water the mix until it is thoroughly moist. Scoop out a hole large enough for the roots of the plant. Gently remove the plant and its potting mix from its original container, and plant it so that the top of the root ball is level with the surface of the mix. Fill the hole with mix, packing it gently around the roots. Pat down the surface and water to fill in any air pockets. Mulch plants with organic compost spread 1 inch deep. Place the container where it receives four hours of sun a day and keep the soil only slightly moist but not soggy.

Feverfew
Chrysanthemum parthenium
❧

What You Need
Container plant
*Container 16 inches in diameter
and 18 inches deep*
Potting mix
*All-purpose, timed-release organic
fertilizer granules*
Organic compost
❧

Growing Conditions
4 hours direct sun
❧

Hardiness
Hardy perennial
❧

Propagation
Self-sown seedlings and divisions
❧

When to Plant
After the last frost
❧

LEMON VERBENA TREE

A simple pinch of the leaf of the lemon verbena tree brings forth a pure and strong perfume—stronger than lemon balm, like the peel of a lemon itself. Imagine some French gardeners sitting on an outdoor terrace, indulging in a tisane of lemon-scented tea, from their lemon verbena tree, of course. Coming from South America, the tree found favor and an appropriate climate in the southern United States. Women there sipped the flavored tea, often iced, balancing a glass and fanning to stir up a breeze on a Southern day. In the South, it was miscalled **vervain**, in the French tradition, and there are many scenes in southern literature where cups or glasses of vervain are passed around in delicate company. ¶ This small tree is tender and dislikes cold weather. Growing it in a container allows you the pleasure of placing it where you walk, always convenient to brush against, or to pluck a fragrant leaf. Hardy down to 10° F, lemon verbena may lose all or part of its leaves as the winter chill hits. If you live in a colder climate, make sure to grow your lemon verbena in a container and move it to a protected area. ¶ **HOW TO DO IT** ¶ Before planting, submerge the transplant in its container in a sink or bucket of water until air bubbles cease to appear. Fill the new container with potting mix to within 2 inches of the rim. Add 1 tablespoon all-purpose, slow-release organic fertilizer granules, and toss with the mix to blend it evenly. Water the mix until it is thoroughly moist. Scoop out a hole large enough for the roots of the plant. Gently remove the plant and its potting mix from its container, and plant it so that the top of the root ball is level with the surface of the mix. Fill the hole with mix, packing it gently around the roots. Pat down the surface and water to fill in any air pockets. Mulch plants with organic compost spread 1 inch deep. Place the container where it will receive four hours of sun a day and keep the soil moist but not soggy.

Lemon Verbena
Aloysia triphylla,
also called *Lippia citriodora*

What You Need
Container plant
Container 16 inches in diameter
and 18 inches deep
Potting mix
All-purpose, slow-release organic
fertilizer granules
Organic compost

Growing Conditions
4 hours direct sun

Hardiness
Tender at 10° F

Propagation
Stem cuttings in the spring

When to Plant
Year-round

CLASSIC ENGLISH LAVENDER

The name lavender comes from the Latin word *lavo*, to wash; the ancient Greeks and Romans used the herb to scent their baths, and in the great halls of medieval fiefdoms aromatic herbs and flowers such as lavender and rosemary were strewn over rush-covered floors. Lavender has long been an ingredient in potpourris and fragrant linen closet bags. A washday tradition in France is the drying of pillowcases in the sun, draped over lavender bushes, so pillows sweeten a night's dreams with scents of lavender and sunshine. There are now many different types of lavender hybrids, but *Lavendula augustifolia* is the classic drying type. ¶ Lavender also resides in the kitchen for making jellies, vinegars, cakes, and even as seasoning for stews. ¶ Lavender grows well in containers. If you place it near your front walkway, you can pinch a leaf to help clear your head after a long day's work. Make sure to water consistently, fertilize, and prune after the plant blooms. If you wish to use the blossoms, cut the bloom stalks in the morning just as the dew has dried, and hang them upside down in a warm, dark place to dry. ¶ **HOW TO DO IT** ¶ Before planting, submerge the transplant in its container in a sink or bucket of water until air bubbles cease to appear. Fill the new container with potting mix to within 2 inches of the rim. Add 1 tablespoon all-purpose, slow-release organic fertilizer granules, and toss with the mix to blend it evenly. Water the mix until it is thoroughly moist. Scoop out a hole large enough for the roots of the plant. Gently remove the plant and its potting mix from its container, and plant it so that the top of the root ball is level with the surface of the mix. Fill the hole with mix, packing it gently around the roots. Pat down the surface and water to fill in any air pockets. Mulch plants with organic compost spread 1 inch deep. Place the container where it receives four hours of sun a day and keep the soil only slightly moist but not soggy.

Lavender
Lavendula augustifolia
❧

What You Need
Container plant
Container 16 inches in diameter
and 18 inches deep
Potting mix
All-purpose, slow-release organic
fertilizer granules
Organic compost
❧

Growing Conditions
4 hours direct sun
❧

Hardiness
Hardy perennial
❧

Propagation
Cuttings in the spring
❧

When to Plant
After the last frost
❧

EDIBLE HEIRLOOM FLOWERS

Flowers in your cooking add a dash of fantasy and a pinch of whimsy that sparks up the routine of meal after meal. *Try these flowers in cooked dishes, in salads, as decorations for dessert plates, or float them in iced drinks. The petals of marigolds can be added to scrambled eggs, cooked with rice, or the whole flower can be floated in lemonade. Johnny-jump-ups strewn around a fresh lettuce salad or arranged around the top of a cake add a dainty touch. Sprinkle petals of calendula or marigold on top of an icy-cold vichyssoise or cucumber soup, or add them to baked breads for confetti bursts of color. ¶ Make sure to place your pots close to the kitchen, so snipping off blossoms is convenient. The more you use these blossoms, the more bloom. You can mingle the plants in pots or grow each separately according to whim. Make sure never to spray the plants with any type of pesticide.* ¶ **HOW TO DO IT** ¶ Before planting, submerge the transplants in their containers in a sink or bucket of water until air bubbles cease to appear. Fill each new container with potting mix to within 2 inches of the rim. Add 1 tablespoon all-purpose, slow-release organic fertilizer granules and toss with the mix to blend evenly. Water the mix until it is thoroughly moist. Scoop out evenly spaced holes (about 2 to 4 inches apart) large enough for the roots of the plants. Gently remove each plant and its potting mix from its original container, and plant it so that the top of the root ball is level with the surface of the mix. Fill the hole with mix, packing it gently around the roots. Pat down the surface and water to fill in any air pockets. Mulch plants with organic compost spread 1 inch deep. Place the containers where they will receive four hours of sun a day and keep the soil moist but not soggy.

Calendula
Calendula officinalis
Johnny-Jump-Up
Viola tricolor
Marigold
Tagetes filifolia
❦

What You Need
18 container plants (three 6-packs)
3 containers, each 12 inches in diameter
and 14 inches deep
Potting mix
All-purpose, slow-release fertilizer granules
Organic compost
❦

Growing Conditions
4 hours direct sun
❦

Hardiness
Tender
❦

Propagation
Seeds
❦

When to Plant
After the last frost
❦

FRAGRANT NICOTIANA

Nicotiana is named for Jean Nicot de Villemain, who introduced tobacco to the French Court in the 1600s. This flowering cousin, fragrant nicotiana, bears only fragrant flowers—and what fragrance! Edna St. Vincent Millay celebrated it in a poem, and anyone who has inhaled the perfume in the night air never forgets it. If you planted nicotiana in a pot, you can move it to a sunny location and appreciate it night after night. There are a number of different varieties, from tall to dwarf. Make sure you look for the old-fashioned types, usually white. Nicotania alata, sometimes labeled N. affinis, which is wonderfully fragrant and suitable for containers, comes from South America. So in all but the mildest climates, grow it as an annual. ¶ Although the seeds are quite small, they start quite easily. Get them going inside in the early spring so you can set the plants outdoors as the weather warms. ¶ **HOW TO DO IT** ¶ Fill the container with potting mix to within 2 inches of the rim. Add 1 tablespoon all-purpose, time-release organic fertilizer granules and toss with the mix to blend evenly. Water the mix until it is thoroughly moist. Space the seeds evenly around the container, about 2 inches apart, covering them with ¼ inch of mix. Pat down the surface and water gently to fill in any air pockets. Place the container where it receives at least four hours of sun a day and keep the soil moist but not soggy. When seedlings emerge, thin them to four plants evenly spaced in the container. Fertilize every month with a soluble organic fertilizer diluted to half strength.

Fragrant Nicotiana
Nicotiana alata 'Grandiflora'
or N. affinis

What You Need
Package of seeds
Container, 16 inches in diameter
and 12 inches deep
Potting mix
All-purpose, slow-release organic
fertilizer granules
Soluble organic fertilizer

Growing Conditions
4 hours direct sun

Hardiness
Tender annual

Propagation
Seed

When to Plant
Early spring

Old-fashioned Pink

Old-fashioned pinks send out waves of spicy perfume, which, once inhaled, are rarely forgotten. On a warm summer evening, walking by the blooming plants is pure aroma therapy. These low-growing perennials adapt successfully to rock walls. Although they need regular watering, they can stand the heat of rock-wall living. Their clumping habit allows them to gracefully flow over the edge of walls. In early summer, the $1/2$-inch-wide pink flowers, borne on 12-inch stems, stand nodding above the gray-green lancelike leaves. Cut back spent blooms to keep the plants looking tidy. In some varieties, this encourages a second flush of bloom. ¶ Choose your pinks carefully, for the modern varieties may not be fragrant. Look for Dianthus chinensis, Chinese pink; D. plumarius, cottage pink; or D. gratianopolitanus, cheddar pink. ¶ **HOW TO DO IT** ¶ In spring, after the last chance of frost, you can safely plant your pinks outside. Before planting, submerge the transplants in their containers in a sink or bucket of water until air bubbles cease to appear. Make sure to prepare the soil properly (see pages 27–30), mixing in the all-purpose, time-release organic fertilizer granules according to the directions on the container. ¶ Space the plants evenly in the planting area. Dig a hole for each plant that is twice as wide and as deep as the container. Gently remove the plant and its potting mix from its container, and plant it in the prepared hole so that the top of the root ball is level with the surface of the soil. Fill the hole with soil, packing it gently around the roots. Pat down the surface, and water to fill in any air pockets. Water weekly until the plants become established, then water every ten days throughout the summer.

Chinese Pink
Dianthus chinensis
Cheddar Pink
D. gratianopolitanus
Cottage Pink
D. plumarius

What You Need
Container plants
All-purpose slow-release organic fertilizer pellets

Growing Conditions
6 hours direct sun

Hardiness
Hardy perennial

Propagation
Seeds or divisions

When to Plant
Spring or summer

HEIRLOOMS
IN A PATCH
OF GROUND

D espite the exalted way—in homage to their long history—that most gardeners view heirloom plants, many heirlooms display the easy growing characteristics of the

common weed. Planted in a perennial bed, they thrive without special treatment or attention. Many do well in a drought-resistant garden, able to tide themselves over the hot summer season with only minimal water. There is something about surviving hundreds of years without fussy requirements that builds stamina— and these plants offer that to you. In these busy times, a plant that simply provides beauty without nagging deserves a spot in your garden. ❧ As always, when setting in new plants, pay special attention to soil preparation. When the soil has added amendments such as organic compost and all-purpose, slow-release organic fertilizer granules, the plants stand up to adverse weather conditions as well as to pests and diseases. Look carefully at spacing, for plants too close together compete for light and nutrition, and those too far apart look foolish and leave the garden bed looking bare and unappealing. The optimal spacing allows the leaves of the plants to just touch when they have grown to maturity. This close spacing creates a microclimate underneath the leaves: The shading keeps moisture in the ground longer, a condition better for the plants. ❧ Mulching the ground as the plants grow is beneficial; it improves the health and performance of plants in a number of ways. The mulch shades the ground, helping to maintain moisture content and a more even ground temperature, keeping the roots from baking in hot weather. As the mulch breaks down, it becomes host for beneficial microorganisms that contribute to the health of the soil and, consequently, the plant. Lastly, when applied 6 to 8 inches deep, mulch helps minimize weeds.

Fuller's Teasel

This migrant plant was brought to America from Europe as a tool for the weaving trade. In medieval times, woven cloth was brushed to raise the fibers. The men who did the work were called fullers, and their tools were brushes made from the seed heads of teasel. Consequently, the descriptive Latin name became fullonum. Colonists brought the same plant to eastern America and it was later used in the great northeastern fabric mills. On the West Coast, the Spanish missionaries brought the plant to California in the late eighteenth century. ¶ Now naturalized on both coasts, these handsome biennial plants grow in abandon. They will make an attractive vertical element at the back of a perennial border. All through the summer, the heads make handsome additions to flower arrangements. In the fall, the heads turn to brown and are often used in dried arrangements. ¶ **HOW TO DO IT** ¶ In spring, after the last chance of frost, you can safely sow your teasels outside. If you prefer, start the seeds indoors four to six weeks before the last frost (see pages 30–33). Make sure to prepare the soil properly (see pages 27–30), mixing in the all-purpose, slow-release organic fertilizer granules according to the directions on the container. ¶ For row planting, drag your finger through the prepared moist soil to create a trough ¼ inch deep. Sow the seeds in the trough, spacing them about 1 inch apart. Cover the trough with soil and pat down firmly. Space the rows 4 inches apart. For bed planting, mound the soil in the prepared planting area to form a square bed that is 2 feet by 2 feet and about 6 inches higher than the normal soil level. Sow seeds evenly over the bed, about 1 inch apart, and cover them with ¼ inch of soil. Pat the soil down firmly. ¶ Water the planting area thoroughly but gently, so the seeds are not disturbed. Keep the soil moist but not soggy. After the seedlings are about 3 inches high, mulch them with 1 inch of organic compost.

Fuller's Teasel
Dipsacus fullonum
❧

What You Need
Package of seeds
All-purpose, slow-release organic fertilizer granules
Organic or homemade compost
❧

Growing Conditions
4 hours direct sun
❧

Hardiness
Hardy
❧

Propagation
Seeds in spring and fall, root divisions in spring
❧

When to Plant
Seeds in spring and fall, divisions in spring
❧

BACHELOR'S BUTTON

Ragged sailor, bluebottle, and cornflower are all nicknames for the flower commonly called bachelor's button. It is easily cared for and rewards the gardener with a long season of bloom. From the first of spring into summer, the annual button-round flowers in blue, white, and pink pop out amid long-fingered leaves. The name cornflower derives from its somewhat weedy presence in the cornfields of Eastern Europe. Yet this plant has long been appreciated in the fanciest gardens. Egyptologists identify it in paintings of the pharaohs' gardens. ¶ Bachelor's buttons like full sun, but they do tolerate a touch of afternoon shade. You can sow the seeds in late fall before the first frosts and they'll come up on their own timing in the spring. Of course, you can also plant them in early spring. ¶ **HOW TO DO IT** ¶ In spring, after the last chance of frost, you can safely sow your bachelor's buttons outside. If you prefer, start the seeds indoors four to six weeks before the last frost (see pages 30–33). Make sure to prepare the soil properly (see pages 27–30), mixing in the all-purpose, slow-release organic fertilizer granules according to the directions on the container. ¶ For row planting, drag your finger in a line through the prepared moist soil to create a trough 1/4 inch deep. Sow the seeds in the trough, spacing them about 2 inches apart. Cover the trough with soil and pat down firmly. Space the rows 4 inches apart. For bed planting, mound the soil in the prepared planting area to form a square bed that is 2 feet by 2 feet and about 6 inches higher than the normal soil level. Sow seeds evenly over the bed, about 2 inches apart, and cover them with 1/4 inch of soil. Pat the soil down firmly. ¶ Water the planting area thoroughly but gently, so the seeds are not disturbed. Keep the soil moist but not soggy. After the seedlings are about 3 inches high, mulch them with 1 inch of organic compost. Stake the plants when they grow over 12 inches high.

Bachelor's button
Centaurea cyanus
❧

What You Need
Package of seeds
All-purpose, slow-release organic fertilizer granules
Organic compost
Stakes
❧

Growing Conditions
4 hours direct sun
❧

Hardiness
Tender annual
❧

Propagation
Seeds
❧

When to Plant
Sow in fall or spring
❧

'Mademoiselle Cécile Brunner' Rose

Many clever gardeners have taken a less-than-charming aspect of the garden and covered it with the soft draping form of this rose. Of course, the sprays falling over a tasteful fence or elegant pergola is an exquisite sight, too. ¶ These old polyanthus roses have so many charming merits it seems astonishing that in the flush of the fancy new hybrids, we almost forgot about them. 'Mademoiselle Cécile Brunner' has the endearing quality of blooming care-free year after year. This rose can spread to thirty feet or more, though with light pruning after blooming, control can be imposed. 'Cécile Brunner' blooms in the spring, and with fertilizing and water may bloom again sporadically throughout the summer. ¶ **HOW TO DO IT** ¶ In early spring, when the ground can be worked, plant your bareroot 'Mademoiselle Cécile Brunner.' Unwrap the plant and let it soak in a bucket for several hours. Dig a hole as deep as the roots of the plant and twice as wide. Angle out the sides of the hole slightly. Build up a cone of soil in the bottom of the hole, and spreading the roots, place the plant so the top of the root ball is even with the level of the soil. Add all-purpose, slow-release organic fertilizer granules according to the directions on the container. Return most of the soil to the planting hole, tamping down firmly as you backfill. Fill the hole with water, repositioning the plant if it sinks down by gently pulling it up level again. Complete filling the hole, creating a watering basin, a raised ring of soil around the plant about 2 feet in diameter. ¶ Do not winter-prune lest you cut off the spring bloom that sets on old and new wood. Prune off interfering branches anytime, cutting back to the main stem, but shape the rose lightly after blooming to contain and structure the plant.

'Mademoiselle Cécile Brunner' Rose
Rosa polyanthus
'Mademoiselle Cécile Brunner'

What You Need
Bareroot or container plant
All-purpose, slow-release organic
fertilizer granules

Growing Conditions
4 hours direct sun

Hardiness
Hardy

Propagation
Cuttings in the fall

When to Plant
Bareroot in spring, container
spring and summer

OLD-FASHIONED HOLLYHOCK

Single-flowered hollyhock spires hedging faded red barns seems to epitomize country living. But hollyhock, with its crepe petals, reveals more than a farm heritage. The plant was beloved by the Chinese courtiers, who celebrated it as a sacred flower in T'ang poetry. Although native to the Mediterranean and Central Asia, hollyhock probably traveled along the Silk Route to China. ¶ The stems hold from twelve to twenty flowers in shades of pure white to yellow, pink to purple. If you find the 9-foot giants a bit too large for your garden, there are dwarf varieties. Sowing the seeds one year in July gives you sturdy plants that overwinter to bloom the next spring. Once established, the clumps continue from year to year. Collect the seeds, or separate the shoots around the stem and propagate them. ¶ **HOW TO DO IT** ¶ In early summer, you can sow your hollyhocks outside. If you prefer, start the seeds indoors in spring (see pages 30–33). Make sure to prepare the soil properly (see pages 27–30), mixing in the all-purpose, slow-release organic fertilizer granules, according to the directions on the container. ¶ For row planting, drag your finger in a line through the prepared moist soil to create a trough 1/2 inch deep. Sow the seeds in the trough, spacing them about 5 inches apart. Cover the trough with soil and pat down firmly. Space the rows 6 inches apart. For bed planting, mound the soil in the prepared planting area to form a square bed that is 4 feet wide by 6 feet long and about 6 inches higher than the normal soil level. Sow seeds evenly over the bed, about 1 inch apart, and cover them with 1/4 inch of soil. Pat the soil down firmly. ¶ Water the planting area thoroughly but gently, so the seeds are not disturbed. Keep the soil moist but not soggy. After the seedlings are about 3 inches high, thin or transplant to 12 inches apart. Mulch them with 2 inches of organic compost. Stake the plants when they grow over 3 feet tall.

Hollyhock
Alcea rosea
❧

What You Need
Package of seeds
All-purpose, slow-release organic fertilizer granules
Organic compost
Stakes
❧

Growing Conditions
6 hours direct sun
❧

Hardiness
Hardy biennials
❧

Propagation
Seeds or plantlets
❧

When to Plant
Early summer
❧

Sunflowers

Sunflowers belong to the Helianthus *genus*, from the Greek helios, sun, and anthus, flower. The flower tracks the sun through the sky, facing east and then west. ¶ *Sunflowers are native to the Americas. In pre-Columbian times, the Incas grew and worshipped the sunflowers, etching their images on temple walls. Native American tribes grind the seeds to make flour.* ¶ *Today, there are many new strains, some short, some multiheaded. When you select your plant, make sure that it is open-pollinated so you can save and reuse the seeds. 'Inca Jewels' is an open-pollinated, multiheaded type. Giant varieties such as 'Russian Mammoth' have the biggest, tastiest seeds.* ¶ *To harvest your sunflowers, cover the flower head with a paper bag or netting to keep out hungry birds. When the seeds have fully formed and the head starts to dry, cut off the head and keep in a warm place so it dries thoroughly.* ¶ **HOW TO DO IT** ¶ In spring, after the last chance of frost, you can safely sow your sunflowers outside. If you prefer, start the seeds indoors four to six weeks before the last frost (see pages 30–33). Make sure to prepare the soil properly (see pages 27–30), mixing in the all-purpose, slow-release organic fertilizer granules according to the directions on the container. ¶ For row planting, drag your finger in a line through the prepared moist soil to create a trough 1 inch deep. Sow the seeds in the trough, spacing them about 6 inches apart. Cover the trough with soil and pat down firmly. Space the rows 18 inches apart. For bed planting, mound the soil in the prepared planting area to form a square bed that is 2 feet by 4 feet and about 6 inches higher than the normal soil level. Sow seeds evenly over the bed, about 6 inches apart, and cover them with 1 inch of soil. Pat the soil down firmly. ¶ Water the planting area thoroughly but gently, so the seeds are not disturbed. Keep the soil moist but not soggy. After the seedlings are about 1 foot high, mulch them with 3 inches of organic compost.

RED VALERIAN

Plants are as prone to fads as Fifth Avenue apparel. Once popular in old gardens, spreading in lush carpets of blushing pink or sheet-white, today red valerian, or as sometimes called in old books, Jupiter's-beard, has been banished to the ignobleness of freeway plantings. Yet in 1614, Girolamo Pini painted them amid the regal tulips, love-in-a-mist, and lily-of-the-valley. In the early 1900s, William Robinson, a garden designer and contemporary of Gertrude Jekyll, planted them to grow in abandon at his home, Gravetye Manor. He and Miss Jekyll revolutionized gardening with, as he put it, a "wild" look in planting beds—in stark contrast to Victorian primness. ¶ Perhaps the plant's easy growth and ability to thrive under the worst conditions make it seem less aristocratic than fussy plants that require endless feeding, pruning, mulching, and spraying. Yet this plant does dislike moldy shade and mucky roots, so a damp position in the shade will never do. Plant it out in full sunshine, with some water to keep it looking spry, though it tolerates drought. The 3-foot-tall plants produce sprays of tiny blossoms in heads tinted rosy pink. There is also a white flowering form, Centranthus alba. The leaves, in an attractive green-blue, are about 4 inches long. Blooming from early summer to autumn, the flowers linger and offer longevity as cut flowers. ¶ Red valerian spreads by root cuttings or seeds planted in the spring or fall. Some gardeners argue that red valerian becomes invasive, but transplanting free seedlings to intended garden beds seems more a blessing than a blight. Ask for divisions or plants from friends. ¶ **HOW TO DO IT** ¶ In spring, after the last chance of frost, you can safely sow your red valerian outside. If you prefer, start the seeds indoors four to six weeks before the last frost (see pages 30–33). Make sure to prepare the soil properly (see pages 27–30), mixing in the all-purpose, slow-release organic fertilizer granules according to the ✒

Red Valerian,
also called **Jupiter's-Beard**
Centranthus ruber

❧

What You Need
Package of seeds
All-purpose, slow-release organic
fertilizer granules
Organic compost

❧

Growing Conditions
6 hours direct sun

❧

Hardiness
Hardy

❧

Propagation
Divisions and seeds

❧

When to Plant
Divisions in spring, seeds spring and fall

❧

directions on the container. ¶ For row planting, drag your finger in a line through the prepared moist soil to create a trough ¼ inch deep. Sow the seeds in the trough, spacing them about 2 inches apart. Cover the trough with soil and pat down firmly. Space the rows 4 inches apart. For bed planting, mound the soil in the prepared planting area to form a square bed that is 2 feet by 2 feet and about 6 inches higher than the normal soil level. Sow seeds evenly over the bed, about 2 inches apart, and cover them with ¼ inch of soil. Pat the soil down firmly. ¶ Water the planting area thoroughly but gently, so the seeds are not disturbed. Keep the soil moist but not soggy. After the seedlings are about 3 inches high, mulch them with 1 inch of organic compost. Decrease watering after the plants have become established.

LOVE-IN-A-MIST

Here is an annual flower with two common names, one of which suits the sentimentalist, love-in-a-mist, and one, the cynic, devil-in-the-bush. ¶ Native to the Mediterranean, this plant has delicate lacy leaves and flowers with pointed petals. In colors of pink, blue, and white, blooms keep producing for weeks. A rich sapphire-blue cultivar, called 'Miss Jekyll', is named for the English garden designer of the early twentieth century who revered old-fashioned flowers. ¶ After flowering, the round seed pods stand out handsomely on the plants. Trim back the spent blossoms to encourage new blooms. Save the pods by letting the whole plant dry while still in the ground, or pull out plants just as they are turning brown in bunches and hang them upside down in brown paper sacks. Some gardeners just let the plants self-seed, pulling up the spent, brown stalks with the autumn cleanup. ¶ **HOW TO DO IT** ¶ In spring, after the last chance of frost, you can safely sow your love-in-a mist outside. If you prefer, start the seeds indoors four to six weeks before the last frost (see pages 30–33). Make sure to prepare the soil properly (see pages 27–30), mixing in the all-purpose, slow-release organic fertilizer granules according to the directions on the container. ¶ For row planting, drag your finger in a line through the prepared moist soil to create a trough $^{1}/_{4}$ inch deep. Sow the seeds in the trough, spacing them about 1 inch apart. Cover the trough with soil and pat down firmly. Space the rows 4 inches apart. For bed planting, mound the soil in the prepared planting area to form a square bed that is 2 feet by 2 feet and about 6 inches higher than the normal soil level. Sow the seeds evenly over the bed, about 1 inch apart, and cover them with $^{1}/_{4}$ inch of soil. Pat the soil down firmly. ¶ Water the planting area thoroughly but gently, so the seeds are not disturbed. Keep the soil moist but not soggy. After the seedlings are about 3 inches high, mulch them with 1 inch of organic compost. Stake the plants when they grow over 12 inches high.

Love-in-a-Mist
Nigella damascena
⊱

What You Need
Package of seeds
All-purpose, slow-release organic
fertilizer granules
Organic compost
Stakes
⊱

Growing Conditions
6 hours direct sun
⊱

Hardiness
Hardy annual
⊱

Propagation
Seeds
⊱

When to Plant
In spring or fall
⊱

BLEEDING HEART

Beloved by the Victorians, this import native to Japan graces the early spring with a chain of blooms that look like pale pink hearts with a flash of dripping white petals, strung on a drooping garland. ¶ Growing contentedly in part shade, bleeding-heart's filmy, fernlike foliage returns each spring after the tubers lie dormant all winter. Bleeding-heart does need moisture, so make sure to give the plant plenty of water all year round, working the soil for good drainage. Without adequate water, the plant goes into its winter state of hibernation, dying down and—since a mature clump can be 2 to 3 feet high and equally wide—leaving a gaping hole in the garden bed. But no matter when it disappears, it always comes back dependably in the spring. ¶ If you tire of winter and want to rush the spring season, dig up a clump, pot it, water it well, and keep it in a 55°F room to force it into early bloom. After it blooms, replant the clump in the garden. Late winter is the best time to divide the plant to increase your supply, or gather the seeds and plant them in autumn. ¶ **HOW TO DO IT** ¶ Before planting, submerge the transplant in its container in a sink or bucket of water until air bubbles cease to appear. Make sure to prepare the soil properly (see pages 27–30), mixing in the all-purpose, time-release organic fertilizer granules according to the directions on the container. ¶ Dig a hole for the plant that is twice as wide and as deep as the container. Gently remove the plant and its potting mix from its container, and set it in the prepared hole so that the top of the root ball is level with the surface of the soil. Fill the hole with soil, packing it gently around the roots. Pat down the surface, and water to fill in any air pockets. Mulch the plant with 2 inches of organic compost. Water weekly until the plants become established, then water to keep the soil moist throughout the summer.

Bleeding Heart
Dicentra spectabilis

What You Need
Container plant
All-purpose, slow-release organic fertilizer granules

Growing Conditions
Part shade

Hardiness
Hardy

Propagation
Seeds or divisions

When to Plant
Plant until July, tubers and seeds in fall

FROM THE
GARDEN TO
THE KITCHEN

Succulent tomatoes, dripping with old-fashioned flavor; watermelons candy sweet and crunchy; or apples with blushing pink flesh—well, these delights can't be found in

supermarkets. Growing your own heirloom fruits and vegetables is the only way to enjoy them because they are too perishable for long-distance shipping and unsuitable for commercial production. ❧ The appearance of heirloom fruits and vegetables is often unusual. For example, some tomatoes are all green when ripe, others streaked with green and orange. Their eccentric good looks intensifies the pleasure of setting them on your table. And wait until you savor the exquisite flavor of fruits and vegetables harvested at their peak—not picked green and ripened by gas. ❧ Leaving the fruits or vegetables on the tree, bush, or vine allows the flavors to fully develop. The minutes it takes for a short walk back to the kitchen can't compare to the days it takes most produce to reach the marketplace. Because these are plants for your family's table, grow them organically, using organic fertilizers and soap-based pesticides to ensure that they are wholesome as well as delicious. ❧ Don't skip this chapter just because you have a small garden. If you have a patio or a terrace that receives four to six hours of sunlight every day, you can grow many of these plants in containers. Even the apple tree can be purchased on dwarf rootstock that takes well to container culture. In small gardens, lettuce can be tucked in between spring annuals, adding color and texture to the perennial bed, and finishing before the plants expand to fill the space in summer. The beans grow on bushes; and with a deep container to accommodate the roots, they will bear a harvest just outside the kitchen door. Remember that plants growing in containers need regular fertilizing and careful attention to watering because there is less root space for the plant to draw nourishment.

BORAGE

Borage's nickname, "cool tankard," makes you wonder about this plant with lovely star-shaped true-blue flowers. An old garden book from the late 1800s describes adding borage leaves to claret cup—which explains its nickname—while the flowers graced salads. Pliny, the ancient Roman author and expert on medicinal plants, recommended eating the leaves in salad for the "exhilarating" experience. One can only guess that he wasn't referring to the fact that the leaves are covered with fine prickles. And stalwart souls other than Pliny are said to eat them—when small—in salads; their flavor mimics cucumbers. ¶ The flowers are often pictured in medieval illuminated manuscripts and used as a motif in now-crumbling embroidery. Pluck the flowers off the hairy stem and scatter them on the top of soups or salads. Or, for summer's cooling ice tea, freeze bright blue blossoms in lemonade ice cubes. ¶ The plant grows quickly, hurriedly bursting into sprays of blossom by the end of spring. Scattering their seed around brings one and even two more harvests. Growing to about 3 feet high and wide, gradually becoming top heavy, they may split and reveal hollow stems. If you live in a mild-winter climate, you can start off a few plants and then sit back with your claret cup as borage plants pop up all over the garden, all year long. In cold winter climates, gather up the seeds in late summer and replant the next spring. ¶ **HOW TO DO IT** ¶ In spring, after the last chance of frost, you can safely sow your borage outside. If you prefer, start the seeds indoors four to six weeks before the last frost (see pages 30–33). Make sure to prepare the soil properly (see pages 27–30), mixing in the all-purpose, slow-release organic fertilizer granules according to the directions on the container. ¶ For row planting, drag ✔

Borage
Borago officinalis
❧

What You Need
Package of seeds
All-purpose, slow-release organic fertilizer granules
Organic compost
❧

Growing Conditions
4 hours direct sun
❧

Hardiness
Tender annual
❧

Propagation
Seeds
❧

When to Plant
In spring and fall
❧

your finger in a line through the prepared moist soil to create a trough $^1/_4$ inch deep. Sow the seeds in the trough, spacing them about 1 inch apart. Cover the trough with soil and pat down firmly. Space the rows 4 inches apart. For bed planting, mound the soil in the prepared planting area to form a square bed that is 2 feet by 2 feet and about 6 inches higher than the normal soil level. Sow seeds evenly over the bed, about 1 inch apart, and cover them with $^1/_4$ inch of soil. Pat the soil down firmly. ¶ Water the planting area thoroughly but gently, so the seeds are not disturbed. Keep the soil moist but not soggy. After the seedlings are about 3 inches high, mulch them with 1 inch of organic compost.

'LUMINA' PUMPKIN

This pumpkin makes a splash as a ghostly carved pumpkin at Halloween, but the flavor of its flesh makes it a star in the kitchen as well. White pumpkins have been around for a long time; in fact, in 1614, Giacomo Castelvetro describes white pumpkins in a book he wrote on Italian fruits, herbs, and vegetables. ¶ You need to make lots of room for 'Lumina' pumpkins. But don't forget you can mix them with corn, as the Native Americans did, or, if hill planting, surround the hill with spring salad greens, which will be long gone by the time the pumpkin gears up to sprawl. ¶ As the pumpkins grow, set the young fruit on hay, cardboard, or even wood to raise it up off the ground and keep the skin out of contact with damp soil. Let the pumpkins dry on the vines, then gather them and store until they are needed in a cool, 60° F location. ¶ Set aside your Halloween jack-o'-lanterns and cook up the rest in soups, pies, and sweet pumpkin puree. ¶ **HOW TO DO IT** ¶ In spring, after the last chance of frost has passed and when the ground has warmed, you can safely sow your pumpkins outside. If you prefer, start the seeds indoors four to six weeks before the last frost (see pages 30–33). Make sure to prepare the soil properly (see pages 27–30), mixing in the all-purpose, slow-release fertilizer granules according to the directions on the container. ¶ For hill planting, mound the soil in the prepared planting area to form a round bed that is 2 feet in diameter and about 6 inches higher than the normal soil level. Sow four seeds on each hill, pushing them down 1 inch deep. Pat the soil down firmly. Thin to the two strongest seedlings when plants are 3 inches high. Leave 10 feet between hills. ¶ Water the planting area thoroughly but gently, so the seeds are not disturbed. Keep the soil moist but not soggy. After the seedlings are about 3 inches high, mulch them with 1 inch of organic compost. Harvest the pumpkins when your fingernail cannot easily pierce the skin, leaving 2 to 4 inches of stem on each pumpkin.

'Lumina' Pumpkin
Curcubita pepo
❧

What You Need
Package of seeds
All-purpose, slow-release organic fertilizer granules
Organic compost
❧

Growing Conditions
Full sun
❧

Hardiness
Tender annual
❧

Propagation
Seed
❧

When to Plant
When the nights do not fall below 50° F
❧

Traditional corn: 'Bloody Butcher', 'Baby Blue', and 'Calico'

Seven thousand years ago, savvy farmers in Mesoamerica began to cross grasses to make a larger and larger seed pod. Columbus mentions corn in his journal after he met the Taino, native inhabitants of the New World. They called the grain mahiz, and throughout most of the world, it is still called maize. The Aztecs, Mayans, and Incas all grew and cooked corn, learning cultivation and preservation techniques and continually crossbreeding to improve it. In time corn spread throughout the Americas, in different shapes and colors used for cooking or popping. ¶ Corn was a sacred food to the Native Americans, and many ceremonies and sacred dances, such as the corn dance of the New Mexico pueblos, still celebrate its life-giving importance. The Iroquois planted corn in hills, letting it grow about half a foot before they started seeds of squash and beans, which used the tall corn as poles to climb. The Zuni ground their blue corn and made thin flat bread called piki. Today, many tribes still make long links of corn to dry in the sun. ¶ When the dried kernels are thrown into winter stews and soups, they soften quickly and provide a sweet, slightly chewy winter vegetable. You can dry 'Bloody Butcher' and grind it to make cornmeal; the red flakes from the dark red kernels will polka-dot the bread made from it. 'Baby Blue' and 'Calico' both make delicious popcorn. ¶ Remember that corn crossbreeds easily. If you plan to save seed, it's best to grow just one variety; to grow more than one, space the varieties far away from each other or bag the ears. 'Bloody Butcher' corn grows about 10 to 11 feet tall; 'Baby Blue' and 'Calico' corn grow to a more reasonable 8 feet. ¶ **HOW TO DO IT** ¶ In spring, after the last chance of frost and when the ground has warmed, you can safely sow your corn outside. If you prefer, start the seeds indoors four weeks before the last frost (see pages 30–33). Make sure to prepare the soil properly (see pages 27–30), mixing in the all-purpose, slow-release organic fertilizer granules according to the directions on the container. ¶ Plant the corn in short rows, making ✒

'Bloody Butcher', 'Baby Blue', 'Calico' Corn
Zea mays 'Bloody Butcher', 'Baby Blue', 'Calico'
⁂

What You Need
Package of seeds
All-purpose, slow-release organic fertilizer granules
Organic high-nitrogen soluble fertilizer
Organic compost
Planting blocks, 6 feet by 6 feet
⁂

Growing Conditions
Full sun
⁂

Hardiness
Tender annual
⁂

Propagation
Seed
⁂

When to Plant
When the nights do not fall below 50° F
⁂

blocks of rows to increase pollination. Drag your finger through the prepared moist soil to create a trough 1^1/$_2$ inches deep. Sow the seeds in the trough, spacing them 4 inches apart with 3 feet between rows. Cover the trough with soil and pat down firmly. After the plants are 6 inches high, thin them to one every foot. ¶ Fertilize the corn when it is 6 to 8 inches high, using a high-nitrogen soluble organic fertilizer according to the directions on the container. Make sure to continue to water regularly and increase watering at the time the tassels emerge from the stalk to ensure good growth of the kernels. Harvest the corn about three weeks after the first silk appears, when milky juice squirts out of a kernel. Cook the corn immediately or dry it for future use by pulling back the husks, stripping off the silk, and hanging the ears in long chains out of the direct sun, in a warm, dry place.

'MOON & STARS' WATERMELON

Moon & Stars' watermelons bring an image of the night sky down to the ground—a deep dark green rind accented by polka dots, golden moons, and smaller pinpoints of stars. It is available with both yellow flesh and red flesh; both have a sweet, rich flavor. ¶ Originating in Africa, watermelons are related to cucumbers. They like warmth, so if your temperatures are on the cool side, try spreading black plastic on top of the ground to raise soil temperatures. Grow your melons in hills of rich soil with lots of water. Reduce watering as melons approach ripeness to create intense flavor and keep the melons from splitting. ¶ To determine ripeness in a melon on the vine, look at the bottom of the melon: A color change from dark green to lighter yellow indicates ripeness. Another ripeness indication is when the tendrils that grow along the stem shrivel. To save the seeds, collect, wash, and dry them for about three to five days, then store. ¶ **HOW TO DO IT** ¶ In spring, after the last chance of frost and when the ground has warmed, you can safely sow your 'Moon & Stars' outside. If you prefer, start the seeds indoors four to six weeks before the last frost (see pages 30–33). Make sure to prepare the soil properly (see pages 27–30), mixing in the all-purpose, slow-release organic fertilizer granules according to the directions on the container. ¶ For hill planting, mound the soil in the prepared planting area to form a round bed that is 2 feet in diameter and about 6 inches higher than the normal soil level. Sow six seeds on each hill, pushing them down 1 inch deep. Pat the soil down firmly. Thin to the three strongest seedlings when they are 3 inches high. Leave 6 feet between hills. ¶ Water the planting area thoroughly but gently, so the seeds are not disturbed. Keep the soil moist but not soggy. After the seedlings are about 3 inches high, mulch them with 1 inch of organic compost.

'Moon & Stars' Watermelon
Citrullus lanatus 'Moon & Stars'

❧

What You Need
Package of seeds
All-purpose, slow-release organic fertilizer granules
Organic compost

❧

Growing Conditions
Full sun

❧

Hardiness
Tender annual

❧

Propagation
Seeds

❧

When to Plant
When the nights do not fall below 50° F

❧

'JACOB'S CATTLE' SHELLING BEANS

Baked beans were once a staple in a pre-super-market time, when meat was reserved for feast days and a bean pot celebrated Sunday dinners. To many people today, dried beans appear time consuming to prepare; first they soak, then they cook. Consequently, more and more dried bean cultivars disappear from garden catalogues every year. Dried beans are actually very practical: They store well in the pantry, always ready to make a great meal. Soaking them overnight in the refrigerator makes them ready to prepare the next day. ¶ Growing dried beans is simple. 'Jacob's Cattle' beans are a bush type, growing only about 2 feet tall and maturing in ninety days. They thrive in a warm soil, so wait till later in the spring to plant them. About six weeks after the plant blossoms, when the dangling pods are just starting to dry, cut off the roots and lift up the whole plant and hang it upside down in a warm, dark place. Shell the beans individually, or place the whole dried bush in a cloth sack and beat it to break the beans out of the pods. Separate out the beans. In some cases, a bean weevil invades, so store the dried beans in an airtight, glass jar and examine them periodically. Beans with tiny round holes in them, or dust in the bottom of the jar indicates an infestation, so empty out the beans, sorting the good from the bad and then reseal. Place the jar in the freezer for five days to kill any remaining bugs. ¶ **HOW TO DO IT** ¶ In spring, after the last chance of frost, and when the soil has warmed, you can safely sow your beans outside. If you prefer, start the seeds indoors four to six weeks before the last frost (see pages 30–33). Make sure to prepare the soil properly (see pages 27–30), mixing in the all-purpose, slow-release organic fertilizer granules according to the directions on the container. ¶ For row planting, drag your finger in a line through the prepared moist 🖝

soil to create a trough 1 inch deep. Sow the seeds in the trough, spacing them about 2 inches apart, thinning to 4 inches when the beans have four sets of leaves. Cover the trough with soil and pat down firmly. Space the rows 18 inches apart. For bed planting, mound the soil in the prepared planting area to form a square bed that is 2 feet by 2 feet and about 6 inches higher than the normal soil level. Sow seeds evenly over the bed, about 2 inches apart, and cover them with $1/4$ inch of soil. Pat the soil down firmly. Thin plants to 4 inches apart when the beans have four sets of leaves. ¶ Water the planting area thoroughly but gently, so the seeds are not disturbed. Keep the soil moist but not soggy. After the seedlings are about 3 inches high, mulch them with 1 inch of organic compost.

Old-fashioned lettuce: 'Deer's Tongue', 'Black-Seeded Simpson', and 'Oakleaf'

"Eat your salad" has been an admonition for a long time—we find tossed salads in the earliest recipe books. The Greeks and Romans stirred up salads, and their wandering, warring armies carried the tradition over Europe. In the earliest days, greens were foraged; now all you need to do is grow them in your garden. ¶ In the old catalogues, these lettuces used to be called cutting lettuces, because their leaves could be cut individually over a period of time, instead of being pulled out as a whole head. This would provide a long season of harvest in a small space. These old types, each with a uniquely shaped leaf, make a salad with superb flavor and sophisticated appearance. You won't find these types in markets or stores, for they don't ship well; their superbly tender leaves would wilt on trips much longer than from the garden to the kitchen. ¶ Lettuces cannot stand too much summer sun; in hot summer climates, interplant them between rows of taller plants so they have some shade during the heat of the day. Consider giving up your old technique of row planting, and plant these varieties thickly in beds, plucking the thinnings for early salads until the maturing plants cover the bed leaf tip to leaf tip. The juicy, succulent lettuces need plenty of water during early growth to keep them growing quickly. Dense growth over the bed helps shade the soil, retaining water to speed the lettuces on their way. To harvest, just cut off the outside leaves. ¶ Try planting successively, sowing a new patch of lettuce every three weeks to keep your salad bowl full of the freshest greens. For the earliest harvest, start some seeds indoors six weeks before the last frost, so you can pop young plants into the ground as soon as it is safe to do so. ¶ **HOW TO DO IT** ¶ In spring, after the last chance of frost, when the soil has warmed, you can safely sow your lettuces outside. If you prefer, start the seeds indoors four to six weeks before the last frost (see pages 30–33). Make sure to prepare the soil properly (see pages 27–30), mixing in the all-purpose, slow-release organic fertilizer granules according to the direc- ✐

'Black-Seeded Simpson', 'Deer's Tongue', 'Oakleaf' Lettuce
Lactuca sativa 'Black-Seeded Simpson', 'Deer's Tongue', 'Oakleaf'
❧

What You Need
Package of seeds
All-purpose, slow-release organic fertilizer granules
Organic compost
❧

Growing Conditions
4 hours direct sun
❧

Hardiness
Tender annual
❧

Propagation
Seed
❧

When to Plant
After the last frost
❧

tions on the container. ¶ For row planting, drag your finger in a line through the prepared moist soil to create a trough $\frac{1}{4}$ inch deep. Sow the seeds in the trough, spacing them about 1 inch apart. Cover the trough with soil and pat down firmly. Space the rows 4 inches apart. For bed planting, mound the soil in the prepared planting area to form a square bed that is 2 feet by 2 feet and about 6 inches higher than the normal soil level. Sow seeds evenly over the bed, about 1 inch apart, and cover them with $\frac{1}{4}$ inch of soil. Pat the soil down firmly. ¶ Water the planting area thoroughly but gently, so the seeds are not disturbed. Keep the soil moist but not soggy. After the seedlings are about 3 inches high, mulch them with 1 inch of organic compost.

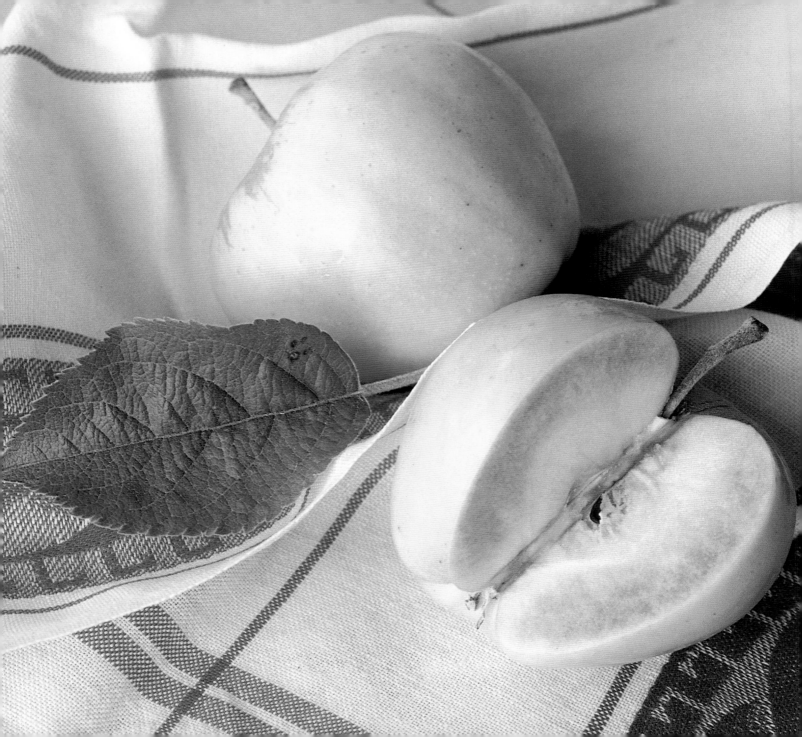

'PINK PEARL' APPLE

The deep-pink flowers predict the later pink-flushed flesh of this extraordinary apple variety. The lovely pink blushes through the pearly, opalescent white skin. ¶ 'Pink Pearl' apples may not be judged quite heirloom, sliding in with a birthday in the 1920s. Bred in Ettersburg, California, the early-season apple can be grown in many mild winter climates; it needs a chill factor of only 600 hours. You do need another apple for cross-pollination, though it doesn't need to be of the same variety, but it does need to bloom about the same time—in early or mid season. You can purchase a tree on different rootstocks, which will affect the height of the plant. A dwarf rootstock limits the tree to about 5 to 7 feet; semi-dwarf, 10 to 12 feet; and standard, to 30 feet. ¶ In late winter, nurseries sell dormant fruit trees as bare-root plants, and many sell plants in containers year-round once the stems have buds. Most mail-order nurseries ship only bare-root fruit trees, so remember to place an order early in the year. ¶ **HOW TO DO IT** ¶ In early spring, when the ground can be worked, plant your bare-root 'Pink Pearl'. Unwrap the plant and let it soak in a bucket for several hours. Dig a hole as deep as the roots of the plant and twice as wide. Angle out the sides of the hole slightly. Build up a cone of soil in the bottom of the hole, and spreading the roots, place the plant so the top of the root ball is even with the level of the soil. On dwarf and semi-dwarf trees, make sure that the grafted bud union is above the soil level but by no more than 1 inch. Add all-purpose, slow-release organic fertilizer granules, according to the directions on the container. Return most of the soil to the planting hole, tamping down firmly as you backfill. Fill the hole with water, repositioning the plant if it sinks down by gently pulling it up level again. Complete filling the hole, and surround the tree with a raised circle of soil about 2 feet in diameter for a watering basin.

'Pink Pearl' Apple
Malus 'Pink Pearl'

What You Need
Bare-root or container plant
All-purpose, slow-release organic
fertilizer granules

Growing Conditions
6 hours direct sun

Hardiness
Hardy

Propagation
Graft cuttings to appropriate root stock

When to Plant
Bare root in spring, container spring
and summer

Many claim that Thomas Jefferson was the first colonist to grow tomatoes in the United States. Other historians allege tomatoes were already widely grown throughout the southern colonies, imported by the Spanish missionary fathers who had eaten them in Central and South America. This historical disagreement aside, the tomato was one of the new American fruits discovered during the Spanish conquest of Central America in the 1500s. After four hundred years of breeding, there are colors, shapes, and tastes for every palette; the ordinary smooth, round red tomato of the market seems dull and uninspired by contrast. Many heirlooms flaunt wild colors, from green, as in the cherry-style 'Green Grape', to the red and orange stripes of 'Mr. Stripey'. 'Costoluto Genovese' grows as a misshapen bumpy tomato, with a great flavor for out-of-hand eating or cooking up in sauces. 'Brandywine' has a superb flavor many feel is the epitome of tomato taste. ¶ These varieties do well in most climates, but don't be surprised if your harvest is lighter with heirlooms than with hybrids. The intense flavor makes up for that, however. Build a wire cage for each plant with a circle of wire 24 inches in diameter and at least 4 feet high, or use a stake, loosely tying the plant to it with cloth strips. Make sure to work lots of organic compost into your planting beds and rotate your plants from year to year as a precautionary step, because these tomatoes are not resistant to soil-borne diseases. ¶ **HOW TO DO IT** ¶ In spring, after the last chance of frost, when the soil has warmed and your plants have three sets of leaves, you can safely plant your tomatoes outside. Make sure to harden them off for a week by leaving them outside in a protected place during the day and bringing them in at night. Before planting, submerge the transplants in their containers in a sink or bucket of water until air bub- ✐

'Brandywine', 'Costoluto Genovese', 'Mr. Stripey', 'Green Grape' Tomatoes
Lycopersicon lycopsersicum
'Brandywine', 'Costoluto Genovese', 'Mr. Stripey', 'Green Grape'

❧

What You Need
3 container plants, bought or grown from seeds
3 square feet prepared ground
Organic low-nitrogen fertilizer
Organic compost
Stakes or wire cages

❧

Growing Conditions
³/₄ to a full day direct sun

❧

Hardiness
Tender annual

❧

Propagation
Seed

❧

When to Plant
When the nights do not fall below 50° F

❧

bles cease to appear. Make sure to prepare the soil properly (see pages 27–30), mixing in the organic low-nitrogen fertilizer according to the directions on the container. ¶ Space the plants evenly in the planting area. Dig a hole for each plant that is twice as wide and as deep as the container. Gently remove the plant and its potting mix from its container, and set it into the prepared hole so that the first set of true leaves is at the soil level. Fill the hole with soil, packing it gently around the roots. Pat down the surface and water to fill in any air pockets. Set up wire cages, stakes, or other supports. ¶ Keep the soil moist but not soggy. After the seedlings are about 6 inches high, mulch them with 1 inch of organic compost.

Mail-order sources

Seed companies test-grow their seeds or work closely with growers contracted to supply seed to them. Although they offer seed to gardeners all over the United States, they can make suggestions on what seeds would do well in your local area. Call the companies closest to you for recommended varieties to grow successfully in your climate. Some companies charge for their catalogue or mail only at certain times of the year. Call or write to check prices and availability.

Abundant Life Seeds
Foundation
P.O. Box 772
Port Townsend, WA 98368
(360) 385-5660
*Catalogue $1,
membership $30 annually*

Bountiful Gardens
18001 Shafer Ranch Road
Willits, CA 95490-9626
(707) 459-6410

Fox Hollow Seed Company
P.O. Box 148
McGrann, PA 16236
(421) 548-SEED
Catalogue $1

Heirloom Garden Seed
Company
P.O. Box 138
Guerneville, CA 95446
(707) 887-9129

Native Seeds/SEARCH
2509 Campbell, #325
Tuscon, AZ 85719
(602) 327-9123

Nichols Garden Nursery
1190 North Pacific Hwy
Albany, OR 97321-45948
(503) 928-9280

North American Fruit
Explorers (NAFEX)
Route 1, Box 94
Champin, IL 62628
(217) 245-7589

Redwood Seed Company
P.O. Box 361
Redwood City, CA 94064
(415) 325-7333

Santa Barbara Heirloom
Seedling Nursery
P.O. Box 4235
Santa Barbara, CA 93140
(805) 968-5444

Seed Savers Exchange
3076 North Winn Road
Decorah, IA 52101
(319) 382-5990

Seeds Blum
HC Idaho City Stage
Boise, ID 83706
(800) 528-3658

Seeds of Change
621 Old Santa Fe Trail, #10
Santa Fe, NM 87501
(505) 438-8080

Seeds of Diversity
P.O. Box 36
Station Q
Toronto, Ontario M4T 2L7
Canada

Shepherd's Garden Seeds
30 Irene Street
Torrington, CT 06790
(203) 482-3638

Southern Exposure Seeds
Exchange
P.O. Box 170
Earlysville, VA 22936
(800) 973-4703

Vintage Gardens
2227 Gravenstein
Highway South
Sebastopol, CA 95472
(707) 829-2035

BIBLIOGRAPHY

Ashworth, Suzanne.
Seed to Seed.
Decora, Iowa: Seed Savers Exchange,
1991

Bremness, Lesley.
The Complete Book of Herbs: A Practical Guide to Growing and Using Herbs.
New York: Viking Studio Books,
a Division of Penguin Books, 1988.

Creasy, Rosalind.
Cooking from the Garden.
San Francisco: Sierra Club Books, 1988.

Hortus Third Dictionary.
New York: Macmillan, 1976.

Jabs, Carolyn.
The Heirloom Gardener.
San Francisco: Sierra Club Books, 1984

Jeckyll, Gertrude.
Wall and Water Gardens.
New York: Scribner and Sons, 1928.

Vilmorin-Andrieux, M. M.
The Vegetable Garden.
London: John Murray, 1885.
Reprinted by the Jeavons-Leler Press,
Palo Alto, 1976.

Viola, Herman J., and Carolyn Margolis,
Editors.
Seeds of Change: Five Hundred Years Since Columbus.
Washington DC: Smithsonian Institution
Press, 1991.

Watson, Benjamin.
Taylor's Guide to Heirloom Vegetables.
Boston: Houghton Mifflin Company,
1996.

INDEX

Acknowledgments

Like the histories of heirloom plants, this book was nurtured and grown with the help of many people along the way. In the beginning, Mickey Choate, Carolyn Larson, and Susan Lescher of the Lescher Agency nurtured the seed of the idea. Jill Appenzeller of Appenzeller Landscape Design, Fredrique Lavoipierre of Shoestring Nursery, Vintage Gardens in Sebastopol, California, Terry and Carolyn Hansen of Sonoma Antique Nursery in Healdsburg, California, and Wendy Krupnik of Shepard's Seeds in Felton, California, provided plants, ideas, and information like water and nourishment for the development of the young project. Faith wants to thank the Susans, Sidney, Catherine and Victoria, Beth, Laurie, Kathy, her friends at the Apple Farm in Anderson Valley, California, her friends at Tantau in St. Helena, California, and the Wags. The main pruner and weeder of the manuscript was Melinda Levine, our editor along with the team at Chronicle Books, Leslie Jonath, Sarah Putman, Julia Flagg, and Amy Torack. Our thanks for the graceful design goes to Aufuldish & Warinner. As ever and ever, our grateful thanks go to those who nurture and sustain us, Bruce Lefavour and Arann and Daniel Harris. Many thanks to Basso and Company of St. Helena, California, for the generous loan of the charming wicker settee on our cover.